THE POWER OF PRAYER

A CHRISTIAN MANIFESTO

ELIJAH M. JAMES, PH.D.

Copyright © 2024

All rights reserved

No part of this book may be reproduced in any form or by any electronic or mechanical means without permission in writing from the author.

Canadian Cataloguing in Publication Data

James, Elijah M.

The Power of Prayer: A Christian Manifesto

ISBN 978-1-0689032-1-2

EJ Publishing

603 White Hills Run

Hammonds Plain

Nova Scotia, Canada B4B 1W7

This book is dedicated to prayer warriors everywhere. May the transformative power of your prayers be experienced worldwide.

TABLE OF CONTENTS

PREFACE 1
    A Special Note on the Prayers in this book 3

INTRODUCTION 6
    The Essence of Prayer 6
    The Call to Prayer 7
    Purpose and Vision of the Manifesto 7
    The Journey Ahead 8
    A Manifesto for Change 9
    Conclusion 9
    Prayer 10

PART 1: FOUNDATIONS OF PRAYER 11
    CHAPTER 1: UNDERSTANDING PRAYER 12
        Opening Prayer 12
        Introduction 13
        Definition and Nature of Prayer 14
        The Biblical Basis for Prayer 15
        Historical Perspectives on Christian Prayer 16
        Conclusion 18
        Closing Prayer 18
    CHAPTER 2: BIBLE VERSES ON PRAYER 20
        Opening Prayer 20
        Introduction 21
        The Bible on Prayer 21
        Conclusion 26

Closing Prayer 26
CHAPTER 3: THE THEOLOGY OF PRAYER 28
Prayer 28
Introduction 29
The Character of God and Prayer 30
Jesus Christ as the Model of Prayer 31
The Role of the Holy Spirit in Prayer 32
The Purpose of Prayer 33
The Power of Prayer 33
The Communal Aspect of Prayer 34
Conclusion 35
Closing Prayer 35

CHAPTER 4: PRAYER IN THE LIFE OF THE BELIEVER 37
Opening Prayer 37
Introduction 38
Personal Relationship with God 39
Daily Devotion and Prayer Life 39
The Transformative Power of Prayer 40
Corporate Prayer and Community 40
Intercessory Prayer 41
Listening Prayer 43
Prayer and Spiritual Warfare 43
Conclusion 44
Closing Prayer 44

CHAPTER 5: PRAYER WITH FAITH 46
Opening Prayer 46
Introduction 47

    The Essence of Praying with Faith 47

    Practical Steps to Praying with Faith 49

    The Impact of Faith-Filled Prayers 50

    Conclusion 51

    Closing Prayer 51

    Word Puzzles 53

PART II: TYPES AND FORMS OF PRAYER 61

CHAPTER 6: ADORATION AND WORSHIP 62

    Opening Prayer 62

    Introduction 63

    Praising God for Who He Is 64

    Scriptural Examples of Worshipful Prayer 64

    Incorporating Worship into Daily Prayer 65

    The Role of the Holy Spirit in Worship 66

    Conclusion 67

    Closing Prayer 67

CHAPTER 7: CONFESSION AND REPENTANCE 69

    Opening Prayer 69

    Introduction 70

    The Importance of Confession 71

    To Whom Should We Confess? 71

    Biblical Confession Prayers 72

    Living a Life of Repentance 76

    Conclusion 77

    Closing Prayer 77

CHAPTER 8: THANKSGIVING AND GRATITUDE 79

    Opening Prayer 79

Introduction 80
Expressing Thanks in Prayer 81
Stories of Thanksgiving in the Bible 82
Cultivating an Attitude of Gratitude 84
Conclusion 85
Closing Prayer 85

CHAPTER 9: SUPPLICATION AND INTERCESSION 87
Opening Prayer 87
Introduction 88
Asking and Receiving 89
Praying for Others – Intercessory Prayer 90
Scriptural Examples of Supplication 91
Conclusion 93
Closing Prayer 93
Word Puzzles 95

PART III: THE PRACTICE OF PRAYER 103

CHAPTER 10: DEVELOPING A PRAYER ROUTINE 104
Opening Prayer 104
Introduction 105
Establishing Regular Prayer Times 106
Creating a Prayer Journal 107
Overcoming Distractions 108
Conclusion 109
Closing Prayer 109

CHAPTER 11: PRAYING WITH SCRIPTURE 111
Opening Prayer 111
Introduction 112

Using the Psalms in Prayer 113
Praying the Promises of God 113
Scripture-Based Prayer Technique 114
Conclusion 115
Closing Prayer 115

CHAPTER 12: PRAYER ON THE SABBATH DAY 117
Opening Prayer 117
Introduction 118
Biblical Foundations of the Sabbath 118
The Role of Prayer on the Sabbath 119
Practical Ways to Incorporate Prayer on the Sabbath 120
Conclusion 121
Closing Prayer 121

CHAPTER 13: PRAYING IN TONGUES 123
Opening Prayer 123
Introduction 124
Biblical Foundations 124
Theological Significance 125
Intercession and Spiritual Warfare 125
Practical Implications 126
Conclusion 127
Closing Prayer 127

CHAPTER 14: PRAYER IN THE WORKPLACE 128
Opening Prayer 128
Introduction 129
The Significance of Prayer in the Workplace 129
Practical Ways to Incorporate Prayer in the Workplace 130

    Addressing Challenges and Considerations 132

    Conclusion... 132

    Closing Prayer 133

CHAPTER 15: CORPORATE PRAYER 134

    Opening Prayer 134

    Introduction 135

    The Power of Praying Together 136

    Organizing Prayer Groups 137

    Church-Wide Prayer Initiatives 138

    Conclusion... 139

    Closing Prayer 139

    Word Puzzles 141

PART IV: CHALLENGES AND GROWTH IN PRAYER ... 149

CHAPTER 16: OVERCOMING PRAYER OBSTACLES 150

    Opening Prayer 150

    Introduction 151

    Doubt and Unbelief 152

    Spiritual Dryness and Discouragement 154

    Dealing with Unanswered Prayers 155

    Conclusion... 157

    Closing Prayer 157

CHAPTER 17: DEEPENING YOUR PRAYER LIFE 159

    Opening Prayer 159

    Introduction 160

    Advanced Prayer Techniques 161

    Contemplative and Meditative Prayer 162

    Experiencing God's Presence 163

Other Ways to Deepen Your Prayer Life 165
Conclusion 165
Closing Prayer 166

CHAPTER 18: SPIRITUAL WARFARE AND PRAYER 168
Opening Prayer 168
Introduction 169
Understanding Spiritual Warfare 170
Conclusion 174
Closing Prayer 175
Word Puzzles 177

PART V: THE IMPACT OF PRAYER 185

CHAPTER 19: PERSONAL TRANSFORMATION THROUGH PRAYER 186
Opening Prayer 186
Introduction. 187
Testimonies of Changed Lives 188
The Role of Prayer in Personal Holiness 189
Growing in Christlikeness 189
Prayer as a Source of Strength and Guidance 190
Conclusion 191
Closing Prayer, ... 191

CHAPTER 20: PRAYER AND COMMUNITY TRANSFORMATION 193
Opening Prayer 193
Introduction 194
Historical Revivals and Prayer Movements 195
Praying for Your Community 196

    Prayer's Role in Social Justice 197
    Other Considerations.. 199
    Conclusion.. 200
    Closing Prayer 201

CHAPTER 21: GLOBAL IMPACT OF PRAYER 203
    Opening Prayer... 203
    Introduction 204
    Praying for the Nations 205
    Missionary Stories and Prayer.. 206
    The Future of Global Prayer Movements............................... 207
    Conclusion... 208
    Closing Prayer 208

CHAPTER 22: PRAYER IN HEAVEN 210
    Opening Prayer... 210
    Introduction 211
    Is Heaven Real? 211
    Biblical Evidence about Prayer in Heaven............................. 211
    Kinds of Prayer in Heaven... 212
    Prayer as Eternal Worship... 213
    Conclusion... 213
    Closing Prayer 214

CONCLUDING REMARKS 215
    Introduction 215
    Recapitulation of Key Points 215
    The Ongoing Call to Prayer 216
    Encouragement for the Journey Ahead 217
    Conclusion... 218

Closing Prayer..218
Word Puzzles..220

APPENDIX: GLOSSARY OF PRAYER TERMS 228
  GLOSSARY..229

PREFACE

Prayer is a timeless and universal practice, transcending cultures, traditions, and epochs. For Christians, prayer is not merely a ritualistic exercise but a profound expression of faith, a means of communion with God, and a powerful tool for personal and communal transformation. "The Power of Prayer: A Christian Manifesto" seeks to explore the multifaceted dimensions of prayer, drawing on biblical teachings, historical insights, and contemporary reflections to offer a comprehensive understanding of this vital spiritual discipline.

In an age characterized by unprecedented technological advancements and rapid social changes, the essence of prayer remains unaltered. It is a sanctuary of stillness amidst the clamour, a source of strength in times of weakness, and a beacon of hope in moments of despair. This book aims to underscore the enduring relevance of prayer in the modern world, affirming its capacity to bring about profound personal growth and societal change.

The title "A Christian Manifesto" reflects our conviction that prayer is not a passive activity but an active, transformative force. It is a declaration of our commitment to living out the teachings of Jesus Christ, fostering a deeper relationship with God, and contributing to the betterment of the world around us. Through prayer, we align ourselves with God's will, seek His guidance, and draw upon His infinite grace and power.

This book is structured to provide both theological insights and practical guidance. We delve into the biblical foundations of prayer, examining the prayers of Jesus, the Apostles, and other pivotal figures in Christian history. We explore the various forms of prayer—supplication, intercession, thanksgiving, and praise—and their respective roles in nurturing a vibrant spiritual life.

Moreover, we address common challenges and misconceptions about prayer, offering strategies to overcome obstacles such as doubt, distraction, and discouragement. We also highlight the communal aspect of prayer, emphasizing the importance of praying together as a church and the impact of collective intercession on local and global scales.

Throughout these pages, you will find testimonies of individuals whose lives have been radically changed through the power of prayer. These stories serve as powerful reminders of God's faithfulness and the incredible potential of prayer to effect change in our lives and the world.

The inclusion of puzzles serves as a unique and engaging tool to deepen the reader's understanding and engagement with spiritual themes. Word puzzles can help reinforce key concepts and terminology related to prayer, scripture, and spiritual practices, offering a creative and interactive way to meditate on these topics. As readers work through the puzzles, they are encouraged to reflect on their knowledge and perhaps explore new dimensions of their faith. Moreover, the meditative and focused nature of solving puzzles can mirror the contemplative aspects of prayer, fostering a quiet, reflective state that enhances the reader's spiritual journey. By integrating puzzles, the book provides a balanced approach to learning, combining intellectual stimulation with spiritual growth.

In writing "The Power of Prayer: A Christian Manifesto," our hope is to inspire a renewed passion for prayer among believers. We invite you to journey with us, to rediscover the depth and breadth of prayer, and to experience its transformative power in your own life. May this book serve as both a guide and a call to action, encouraging you to embrace the discipline of prayer with fervour and faith.

As you turn these pages, may you encounter the boundless love and power of God, and may your life be enriched and empowered by the practice of prayer.

A Special Note on the Prayers in this book

We believe that prayer is a serious conversation between God and the believer. God is not impressed by grammar and syntax, sentence structure, vocabulary, and flowery language. Communicate with Him with a contrite heart. However, there are many reasons why we have included actual prayers in this book.

Illustrative Examples

Prayers provide concrete examples of how to structure and express prayers, offering readers models they can emulate or adapt to their own situations. These examples can demonstrate different types of prayer, such as adoration, confession, thanksgiving, and supplication.

Instruction and Guidance

Including prayers in a book about prayer can offer guidance on the language, tone, and content appropriate for various prayer contexts. It helps readers understand how to approach God with their needs, praise, confessions, and gratitude, aligning their prayers with biblical principles and theological insights discussed in the book.

Spiritual Inspiration

Prayers can inspire readers by showcasing heartfelt, sincere communication with God. These examples can stir the readers' own desire for deeper communion with God and encourage them to pursue a more vibrant prayer life.

Encouragement and Comfort

The prayers in this book can offer encouragement and comfort to readers. They can resonate with readers' experiences, providing words to express emotions or situations they might struggle to articulate on their own. This can be particularly powerful in times of distress or uncertainty.

Community and Unity

The prayers can foster a sense of community and unity among readers, as they share in the same expressions of faith and supplication. This collective aspect can be particularly poignant in communal or global prayers, uniting readers in a common spiritual endeavour.

Practical Application

Prayers offer a practical application of the concepts discussed in the book, moving from theory to practice. They help readers integrate what they have learned into their daily prayer routines, making the book's teachings more tangible and actionable.

Enhancing Devotional Life

Prayers can enhance the reader's devotional life by providing ready-made prayers for different occasions, such as morning and evening prayers, prayers for specific needs, or prayers for special occasions. This helps readers incorporate structured prayer into their daily spiritual practices.

Reflection and Meditation

These prayers can also serve as a tool for reflection and meditation. Readers can ponder the words of the prayers, allowing them to sink in and facilitate deeper personal reflection and spiritual growth.

Encouraging Specific Prayer Focus

Prayers can direct readers' focus to specific themes or issues, such as praying for the nation, for personal holiness, for community transformation, or for global missions. This focused approach helps readers expand their prayer horizons and intercede for broader concerns beyond their immediate needs.

By incorporating these prayers, this book becomes a comprehensive guide that not only teaches about prayer but also actively engages the reader in the practice of prayer, thereby fostering a richer, more dynamic prayer life.

INTRODUCTION

Prayer is at the heart of the Christian faith. It is the lifeline that connects believers to the divine, a source of solace and strength, and a means of transforming both the individual and the world. In "The Power of Prayer: A Christian Manifesto," we embark on a journey to explore the profound significance of prayer in the life of a Christian, uncovering its power to bring about spiritual renewal and societal change.

The Essence of Prayer

At its core, prayer is an intimate conversation with God. It is an act of worship, a declaration of dependence, and a channel through which we express our deepest desires, fears, and gratitude. Throughout the Bible, prayer is depicted as a fundamental practice, from the fervent prayers of the prophets to the heartfelt petitions of the Psalms, and most notably, the prayers of Jesus Christ Himself.

Prayer is not limited by time or place; it transcends circumstances and reaches into the very presence of God. It is both personal and communal, encompassing private moments of reflection and collective acts of intercession. Through prayer, we align our hearts with God's will, seeking His guidance and intervention in every aspect of our lives.

The Call to Prayer

In today's fast-paced and often chaotic world, the need for prayer has never been more urgent. We are bombarded with challenges and distractions that can easily pull us away from our spiritual foundations. Yet, it is precisely in these moments of uncertainty that prayer becomes our anchor, grounding us in God's unchanging love and power.

"The Power of Prayer: A Christian Manifesto" is a call to return to this vital practice with renewed fervor and commitment. It is an invitation to rediscover the transformative potential of prayer, both individually and collectively. As we delve into the pages of this book, we will uncover the rich heritage of prayer within the Christian tradition and explore practical ways to integrate it into our daily lives.

Purpose and Vision of the Manifesto

The purpose of "The Power of Prayer: A Christian Manifesto" is twofold: to reignite a passion for prayer among believers and to underscore its profound impact on our personal lives and society. This manifesto is a declaration of the indispensable role of prayer in the Christian journey, urging us to cultivate a disciplined and heartfelt prayer life.

Purpose

Reinvigorate Personal Prayer Life: Encourage individuals to develop a consistent and meaningful prayer practice that deepens their relationship with God.

Promote Communal Prayer: Foster a culture of collective prayer within churches and communities, recognizing the power of united intercession.

Equip Believers: Provide practical tools, biblical insights, and strategies to help believers overcome obstacles to effective prayer.

Inspire Action: Show how prayer can lead to tangible actions that reflect God's love and justice in the world.

Vision

Spiritual Renewal: Envision a revival of faith and fervour among Christians, marked by a deep commitment to prayer and dependence on God.

Transformed Lives: See individuals experience profound personal transformation as they encounter God's presence and guidance through prayer.

Unified Church: Imagine a global church united in prayer, interceding for each other and the world, and witnessing the power of collective petition.

Social Impact: Anticipate a world where prayer inspires believers to engage in acts of compassion, justice, and mercy, effecting positive change in their communities and beyond.

The Journey Ahead

This book is structured to guide you through a comprehensive exploration of prayer. We begin by examining the Biblical foundations, looking at how prayer is portrayed in the Old and New Testaments. We will study the prayers of Jesus, who not only taught His disciples how to pray but also modeled a life of deep and consistent communion with the Father.

From there, we will explore the various forms of prayer, understanding how each type—supplication, intercession, thanksgiving, and praise—plays a unique role in our spiritual growth. Practical strategies and insights will be provided to help you overcome common obstacles to effective prayer, such as doubt, distraction, and discouragement.

Moreover, we will highlight the communal aspect of prayer, emphasizing the power of praying together as a church and the impact of collective intercession on both local communities and global issues. Through inspiring testimonies and historical examples, we will see how prayer has been a driving force behind significant spiritual awakenings and social transformations.

A Manifesto for Change

This book is not merely a theoretical treatise on prayer; it is a manifesto for change. It challenges us to take prayer seriously, to prioritize it in our lives, and to recognize its potential to bring about real and lasting change. Whether you are a seasoned prayer warrior or new to the practice, "The Power of Prayer: A Christian Manifesto" aims to inspire and equip you to engage in prayer with passion and purpose.

As you read through these pages, my hope is that you will be encouraged to deepen your relationship with God through prayer. May you experience the peace that comes from resting in His presence, the joy of witnessing His answers, and the power of partnering with Him to effect change in the world. Let this book be a guide and a catalyst for a renewed commitment to the practice of prayer.

Conclusion

Prayer is a gift, a privilege, and a powerful tool. It connects us to the heart of God and empowers us to live out our faith with boldness and compassion. "The Power of Prayer: A Christian Manifesto" is a call to embrace this gift with fervour, to recognize its significance, and to harness its potential for personal and societal transformation. Join me on this journey of discovery and renewal, and let us together unlock the power of prayer in our lives and in our world.

Prayer

Our Heavenly Father,

As we embark on this journey through "The Power of Prayer," we humbly come before You, seeking Your presence, guidance, and wisdom. We acknowledge that prayer is a divine gift, a sacred conversation with You, the Creator of all things. We thank You for the privilege of entering into Your presence, for the assurance that You hear our prayers, and for the promise that You are always with us.

Lord, we ask that You open our hearts and minds as we read and reflect on the pages of this book. Help us to understand the depth and breadth of prayer, to grasp its transformative power, and to recognize its importance in our daily lives. May the insights and truths shared within these chapters draw us closer to You and ignite a passion for prayer that burns brightly within us.

Guide us, Lord, to a deeper relationship with You. Teach us to pray with faith, fervour, and persistence. May our prayers be aligned with Your will and purpose, bringing glory to Your name and advancing Your kingdom here on earth.

We pray for everyone who reads this book, that he or she may be encouraged, strengthened, and inspired. May this journey through the power of prayer lead to personal transformation, renewed hope, and a greater understanding of Your love and grace.

We dedicate this book to Your sincere and faithful **Prayer Warriors**, *Lord, asking that it be a tool in Your hands to bless, uplift, and transform lives. May Your Holy Spirit move through every word, touching hearts and minds, and leading us into a deeper communion with You.*

In the name of Jesus Christ, our Saviour and Lord, we pray.

Amen.

PART 1

FOUNDATIONS OF PRAYER

CHAPTER 1
UNDERSTANDING PRAYER

Through prayer, we communicate with God.

Opening Prayer

Heavenly Father,

As we begin this chapter on "Understanding Prayer," we come before You with open hearts and minds, eager to learn more about this sacred practice. We thank You for the privilege of prayer, for the opportunity to communicate with You, and for the assurance that You hear us.

Lord, we ask for Your wisdom and insight as we delve into the depths of what prayer truly is. Help us to grasp the significance of prayer in our lives and to understand its power and purpose. Open our eyes to see prayer not just as a duty, but as a precious gift and a vital connection with You.

Holy Spirit, be our guide and teacher. Illuminate the scriptures and truths we will explore in this chapter. Reveal to us the beauty of a life rooted in prayer and the profound impact it can have on our relationship with You, ourselves, and others.

Remove any misconceptions or barriers that hinder our understanding of prayer. Grant us the humility to learn and the desire to grow in our prayer lives. May this chapter inspire us to deepen our commitment to prayer and to seek You more earnestly in all things.

Lord, as we embark on this journey of understanding prayer, may our hearts be transformed and our faith strengthened. Let our time spent in this chapter draw us closer to You, filling us with a renewed sense of awe and reverence for the incredible gift of prayer.

In the precious name of Jesus Christ, our Lord and Saviour, we pray.

Amen.

Introduction

Prayer is one of the most profound and essential aspects of the Christian faith, yet it often remains a mystery to many believers. Despite being a cornerstone of our spiritual lives, understanding prayer can sometimes be challenging. What exactly is prayer? How does it work? Why is it so important? These are questions that resonate with many Christians seeking to deepen their relationship with God.

In this chapter, "Understanding Prayer," we will delve into the essence and significance of this sacred practice. Prayer is not merely a religious ritual or a list of requests we present to God; it is a dynamic, transformative dialogue with the Creator of the universe. It is an invitation to commune with God, to align our hearts with His, and to experience His presence, power, and love in profound ways.

We will explore the different dimensions of prayer, from its nature, its biblical foundations, and historical perspectives to its transformative power. By unpacking these elements, we aim to demystify prayer and provide practical insights to enrich your prayer life.

Whether you are a seasoned prayer warrior or just beginning your journey of prayer, this chapter is designed to deepen your understanding and appreciation of this vital spiritual discipline. As we embark on this exploration, may you be inspired to engage more deeply with God through prayer, experiencing its power to transform your life and draw you closer to Him.

Let us open our hearts and minds to the profound truth that prayer is not just about what we say to God, but about the relationship we cultivate with Him. It is an ongoing conversation that invites us into a deeper intimacy with our Heavenly Father, shaping us to become more like Christ and aligning our lives with His divine purposes.

Join us as we embark on this journey of understanding prayer, unlocking its mysteries, and embracing its transformative power in our walk with God.

Definition and Nature of Prayer

Prayer is a fundamental aspect of the Christian faith, a means by which believers communicate with God. It is both a personal and communal act that encompasses praise, thanksgiving, confession, and supplication. Prayer is not merely a ritualistic practice but a dynamic and relational dialogue with the Creator.

At its core, prayer is an expression of dependence on and trust in God. It is through prayer that believers seek guidance, strength, and wisdom, aligning their will with God's divine purposes. Prayer transcends the boundaries of spoken words, embracing silence, contemplation, and the inner longing of the heart.

The nature of prayer is multifaceted. It can be spontaneous or structured, individual or corporate, silent or vocal. Regardless of its form, the essence of prayer lies in its intentionality and sincerity. It is an act of faith, an acknowledgment of God's sovereignty, and a means of nurturing a deeper relationship with Him.

The Biblical Basis for Prayer

The Bible provides a rich tapestry of teachings and examples that underscore the importance and power of prayer. From Genesis to Revelation, prayer is depicted as a vital component of the believer's life.

Old Testament Foundations

Prayer is evident from the earliest narratives of Scripture. Abraham interceded for Sodom and Gomorrah (Genesis 18:22-33), Moses conversed with God on Mount Sinai (Exodus 33:11), and Hannah prayed fervently for a child (1 Samuel 1:10-11). The Psalms, often referred to as the prayer book of the Bible, are filled with heartfelt prayers of lament, praise, and supplication.

New Testament Teachings

The Lord's Prayer

In the New Testament, Jesus provides a model for prayer in what is commonly known as the Lord's Prayer (Matthew 6:9-13; Luke 11:2-4). This prayer encapsulates key elements of prayer:

Adoration:	"Hallowed be your name"
Submission:	"Your kingdom come"
Petition:	"Give us today our daily bread"
Confession:	"Forgive us our debts"
Deliverance:	"Lead us not into temptation".

Apostolic Teachings

The apostles emphasized the significance of prayer in the early church. Paul exhorted believers to "pray without ceasing" (1 Thessalonians

5:17) and to present their requests to God with thanksgiving (Philippians 4:6). James highlighted the power of righteous prayer, stating, "The prayer of a righteous person is powerful and effective" (James 5:16).

Historical Perspectives on Christian Prayer

Throughout church history, prayer has been a central practice, shaping the faith and spirituality of believers across generations.

Early Church and Monasticism

In the early church, prayer was integral to communal worship and personal devotion. The Didache, an early Christian manual, instructed believers to pray the Lord's Prayer three times a day. The rise of monasticism further emphasized the discipline of prayer. Monks and nuns devoted themselves to a life of prayer, meditation, and contemplation, establishing fixed hours for communal prayer known as the Liturgy of the Hours or Divine Office.

Medieval Mysticism

The medieval period saw the flourishing of mystical prayer practices. Figures such as St. Teresa of Ávila and St. John of the Cross explored the depths of contemplative prayer, seeking intimate union with God. Their writings, including "The Interior Castle" and "The Dark Night of the Soul," continue to inspire and guide those pursuing a deeper prayer life.

Reformation and Beyond

The Reformation brought about significant changes in Christian prayer practices. Reformers like Martin Luther and John Calvin emphasized the priesthood of all believers, encouraging personal prayer and direct access to God. The Puritans further stressed the importance of heartfelt, sincere prayer, free from rote repetition.

Modern Movements

In the modern era, prayer has continued to evolve within various Christian traditions. Charismatic and Pentecostal movements have emphasized the role of the Holy Spirit in prayer, including speaking in tongues and prophetic intercession. Contemplative prayer practices have also experienced a resurgence, drawing from ancient traditions to foster a deeper, more reflective approach to communion with God.

The Transformative Power of Prayer

Prayer is not only a means of communication with God but also a transformative practice that shapes the believer's character and faith. Through prayer, individuals experience spiritual growth, greater intimacy with God, and a heightened awareness of His presence and guidance in their lives.

Personal Transformation

Prayer cultivates humility, gratitude, and reliance on God. It helps believers confront their weaknesses, seek forgiveness, and grow in virtues such as patience, love, and compassion.

Community Building

Corporate prayer fosters unity and strengthens the bonds within the Christian community. It allows believers to support and uplift one another, bearing each other's burdens and rejoicing in each other's blessings.

Missional Impact

Prayer fuels the mission of the church, empowering believers to engage in evangelism, social justice, and acts of service. It aligns the church's mission with God's kingdom purposes, seeking His will to be done on earth as it is in heaven.

Conclusion

Understanding prayer is essential for a vibrant Christian life. It is a practice rooted in biblical teachings, enriched by historical traditions, and vital for personal and communal transformation. As believers, embracing the discipline of prayer allows us to deepen our relationship with God, align our lives with His will, and participate in His redemptive work in the world. Through prayer, we are invited into a profound and ongoing conversation with the Creator, Sustainer, and Redeemer of all things.

Closing Prayer

Heavenly Father,

We thank You for the insights and understanding we have gained about prayer in this chapter. Thank You for revealing to us the depth and beauty of this sacred practice. We acknowledge that prayer is a gift, a lifeline that connects us to You, our Creator and Sustainer.

Lord, as we close this chapter, we ask that You seal these truths in our hearts. Help us to remember that prayer is not just about the words we speak, but about the relationship we cultivate with You. Teach us to pray with sincerity, faith, and persistence, always seeking to align our hearts with Yours.

May the understanding we have gained inspire us to deepen our prayer lives. Let us approach Your throne with confidence, knowing that You hear us and that You delight in our prayers. Guide us to be people of prayer, interceding for ourselves, our loved ones, and the world around us.

We ask for Your Holy Spirit to continue to teach us, to lead us into a deeper intimacy with You, and to transform us through our times of prayer. May our prayers be a reflection of our love for You and our desire to see Your will done on earth as it is in heaven.

Thank You, Lord, for the privilege of prayer. We commit ourselves to growing in this practice, trusting that through it, we will draw closer to You and become more like Christ.

In Jesus' name, we pray.

Amen.

CHAPTER 2
BIBLE VERSES ON PRAYER

Pray and He will answer.

Opening Prayer

Heavenly Father,

We come before You with hearts open and minds ready to receive Your word. As we delve into the sacred scriptures, we seek to understand the power and purpose of prayer as revealed in Your holy book. Grant us the wisdom to comprehend the depth of Your teachings and the grace to apply them in our daily lives.

Illuminate our understanding, Lord, and draw us closer to You through the verses we explore. May these scriptures inspire us to cultivate a deeper, more intimate relationship with You, fostering a life of continual communion and unwavering faith.

In Jesus' name, we pray,

Amen.

Introduction

Prayer is a cornerstone of the Christian faith, serving as a direct line of communication between believers and God. The Bible offers a profound exploration of prayer's significance, presenting it not just as a religious duty but as a deeply personal and transformative practice. From the heartfelt laments of the Psalms to the earnest petitions of the New Testament, Scripture is rich with examples and teachings on prayer that reveal its power to shape lives and foster an intimate relationship with God. This chapter delves into these biblical insights, illuminating how prayer can guide, comfort, and empower believers in their spiritual journey

The Bible on Prayer

Here are some verses that reveal the Bible's perspective on prayer.

Psalm 145:18
"The Lord is near to all who call on him, to all who call on him in truth."

Comment: Here we have the assurance that our prayers are not wasted. As long as we call on Him, He is near to us. This assurance is not given to some of us but to all of us.

2 Chronicles 7:14
"If my people, who are called by my name, will humble themselves and pray and seek my face and turn from their wicked ways, then I will hear from heaven, and I will forgive their sin and will heal their land."

Comment: This is a conditional promise to God's people. It's a call to humility, repentance, and a promise of forgiveness and healing. It speaks to the power of individual and collective prayer.

Jeremiah 29:12
"Then you will call on me and come and pray to me, and I will listen to you."

Comment: When we make an effort to seek God in prayer, He will pay attention to us. To call, come, and pray is an expression of faith.

1Kings 8:28
"Yet give attention to your servant's prayer and his plea for mercy, Lord my God. Hear the cry and the prayer that your servant is praying in your presence this day."

Comment: In this prayer of supplication, Solomon implores God for mercy and pleas to God to hear him. Notice his humility before God.

Psalm 17:1
"Hear me, Lord, my plea is just; listen to my cry. Hear my prayer— it does not rise from deceitful lips."

Comment: David cries out to God to listen to his cry and hear his prayer which is sincere and just and in no way pretentious.

1 Chronicles 16:11
"Look to the Lord and his strength; seek his face always."

Comment: This is an admonition to reach out in prayer to God in prayer, and a recognition of His power and might. We are to pray to Him not only when we are in need or trouble but at all times.

Matthew 7:7
"Ask and it will be given to you; seek and you will find; knock and the door will be opened to you."

Comment: This passage of scripture informs us that prayer is not passive but active. Praying does not mean waiting passively for God's will to be done in your life. True, the Bible tells us to "Wait on the Lord" (Psalm 27:14), but while we are waiting, we should be asking, seeking, and knocking.

James 1:5
"If any of you lacks wisdom, you should ask God, who gives generously to all without finding fault, and it will be given to you."

Comment: I have yet to find someone who despises wisdom, but I do know many people who would pay dearly for wisdom. This verse advises us that all we need to do to acquire wisdom is to ask God, and He will give generously, without judging us.

Ephesians 1:18
"I pray that the eyes of your heart may be enlightened so that you may know what is the hope to which he has called you…"

Comment: In this verse, Paul mentions an inner enlightenment that enables us to understand the purpose for which God has called us. As long as the eyes of our hearts are illuminated, we can safely follow our hearts

James 5:14-15
"Is anyone among you sick? Let them call the elders of the church to pray over them and anoint them with oil in the name of the Lord. And the prayer offered in faith will make the sick person well; the Lord will raise them up. If they have sinned, they will be forgiven."

Comment: In this verse, James outlines the procedure to be followed if a believer was sick. The importance of intercessory prayer is highlighted, and the power is prayer is noted. The role of anointing with oil in the healing procedure should be observed.

Mark 11:24
"Therefore I tell you, whatever you ask for in prayer, believe that you have received it, and it will be yours."

Comment: This verse emphasizes the crucial importance of belief in our prayer requests. We must believe that God will grant our prayer requests and He will.

3 John 1:2
"Dear friend, I pray that you may enjoy good health and that all may go well with you, even as your soul is getting along well."

Comment: This short but profound prayer of John emphasizes the close relationship between physical well-being and inner peace and prosperity. We must attend to our physical as well as our spiritual state.

1 John 1:9
"If we confess our sins, he is faithful and just and will forgive us our sins and purify us from all unrighteousness."

Comment: This verse teaches us that forgiveness and purification are dependent upon confession. We can count on God's faithfulness to forgive us of our transgressions, but we must first confess'

Acts 8:22
"Repent of this wickedness and pray to the Lord in the hope that he may forgive you for having such a thought in your heart."

Comment: Have you ever had a sinful thought? Most of us have. Even though we may not act upon them, Peter admonishes us in this verse to turn away from wicked thoughts and ask for forgiveness.

Luke 18:13
"But the tax collector stood at a distance. He would not even look up to heaven, but beat his breast and said, 'God, have mercy on me, a sinner.'"

Comment: In this verse, we see humility, an admission of guilt, remorse, and a plea for mercy. The same is required of us.

1 Timothy 2:1
"I urge, then, first of all, that petitions, prayers, intercession and thanksgiving be made for all people—"

Comment: The truth is, all have sinned (Romans 3:23). In the verse above, Paul urges us all to offer prayers of petition, intercession, and thanksgiving for people globally. We must pray for people we don't know.

Philippians 4:6

"Do not be anxious about anything, but in every situation, by prayer and petition, with thanksgiving, present your requests to God."

Comment: Why worry when you can pray seems to be Paul's message here. A better option seems to be to present our requests to God through prayer. Trust in God is revealed through less worry. Paul reminds us not to forget to give thanks.

Colossians 4:2

"Devote yourselves to prayer, being watchful and thankful."

Comment: Prayer is a serious matter. It is not a wishy-washy activity. We must approach prayer with diligence and sincerity. Thanksgiving should be a part of your prayer.

John 14:13

"And I will do whatever you ask in my name, so that the Father may be glorified in the Son."

Comment: This verse is another classic example of the power of prayer. The power of prayer is unleashed when we ask in the name of Jesus. The purpose is for the Father to be glorified in the Son.

Acts 12:5

"So Peter was kept in prison, but the church was earnestly praying to God for him."

Comment: Prayer was an essential aspect of the life of the early church. Intercessory prayer produced results then, and it will produce results now also. Peter was miraculously released.

Romans 12:12

"Be joyful in hope, patient in affliction, faithful in prayer."

Comment: What does it mean to be faithful in prayer? Being faithful in prayer means maintaining a consistent and devoted prayer life, regardless of circumstances. Being faithful in prayer is about building and sustaining a close, personal relationship with God, making Him a central part of your life through continual, heartfelt communication.

Mark 1:35

"Very early in the morning, while it was still dark, Jesus got up, left the house and went off to a solitary place, where he prayed."

Comment: By this action, Jesus taught an important lesson. We must spend time alone with the Father in prayer. Spending time in solitude with the Father in prayer gives us the necessary spiritual food for our Christian

journey.

Conclusion

As we conclude our exploration of the Bible's teachings on prayer, we are reminded that prayer is more than a spiritual discipline; it is the lifeblood of a vibrant faith. Through the Scriptures, we have seen how prayer fosters intimacy with God, providing solace, guidance, and strength in every circumstance. The biblical examples and teachings challenge us to deepen our prayer lives, approaching God with humility, persistence, and trust. Let us take these lessons to heart, allowing the timeless wisdom of the Bible to transform our prayers into powerful encounters with the Divine, continually drawing us closer to the heart of God and aligning our lives with His purpose.

Closing Prayer

Heavenly Father,

As we close this chapter and reflect on the wisdom of Your Word, we are reminded of the power and significance of prayer in our lives. Thank You for the guidance and inspiration found in these sacred scriptures.

We ask that the truths we have learned take root in our hearts, transforming our approach to prayer. May we be steadfast in seeking Your presence, confident in Your promises, and faithful in our devotion.

Help us to cultivate a deeper relationship with You through earnest and sincere prayer. Strengthen our faith, renew our spirits, and draw us closer to Your divine will. Let our prayers be a reflection of our trust in Your goodness and mercy.

In every season, may we remember to turn to You, knowing that You hear us, care for us, and answer us according to Your perfect wisdom.

In Jesus' name, we pray,

Amen.

CHAPTER 3

THE THEOLOGY OF PRAYER

When we pray, we communicate with the Father.

Prayer

Gracious and Almighty God,

As we begin this chapter on "The Theology of Prayer," we come before You with reverence and humility, eager to explore the profound truths of how prayer reflects Your nature and Your will. We thank You for the gift of prayer and the opportunity it affords us to commune with You, our Creator and Sustainer.

Lord, we ask for Your guidance and enlightenment as we delve into the theology of prayer. Open our hearts and minds to understand the deep spiritual principles and the divine mystery of communicating with You. Help us to grasp the significance of prayer in the context of Your sovereignty, love, and purpose for our lives.

Holy Spirit, be our teacher and guide as we study the theological foundations of prayer. Illuminate the scriptures and reveal to us the heart of God in our times of prayer. Help us to see how prayer aligns us with Your will and draws us into a deeper relationship with You.

Remove any preconceived notions or misunderstandings that may cloud our understanding. Grant us the wisdom to discern Your truth and the humility to accept it. May this chapter inspire us to approach prayer with a greater sense of awe, trust, and devotion.

Lord, as we embark on this journey through the theology of prayer, may our faith be enriched and our relationship with You be strengthened. Let our time in this chapter deepen our understanding of who You are and the incredible privilege we have in being able to speak with You.

In the precious name of Jesus Christ, our Lord and Saviour, we pray.

Amen.

Introduction

The theology of prayer delves into the understanding of prayer within the Christian faith, exploring its significance, purpose, and the divine relationship it fosters. This chapter will examine the theological underpinnings of prayer, focusing on six key areas: the character of God and prayer, Jesus Christ as the model of prayer, the role of the Holy Spirit in prayer, the purpose of prayer, the power of prayer, and the communal aspect of prayer. These themes provide a comprehensive framework for understanding how prayer is both a divine gift and a spiritual discipline.

The Character of God and Prayer

Prayer begins with an understanding of the character of God. The way we perceive God profoundly influences how we approach Him in prayer. The Bible reveals various aspects of God's character that invite us into a deeper prayer life.

God as Loving Father

One of the most comforting and foundational images of God in the Bible is that of a loving Father. In the Lord's Prayer, Jesus teaches His disciples to address God as "Our Father" (Matthew 6:9). This intimate term underscores a relationship based on love, care, and accessibility. Knowing God as a loving Father encourages believers to approach Him with confidence, knowing that He hears and responds to our prayers with compassion and wisdom.

God as Sovereign King

God's sovereignty is another critical aspect of His character. He is the King of kings and the Lord of lords, ruling over all creation with authority and power. This understanding shapes our prayers, reminding us of God's ability to intervene in any situation. It also calls us to submit to His will, trusting that His plans and purposes are perfect and just.

God as Faithful Provider

Throughout Scripture, God is depicted as a faithful provider who meets the needs of His people. In the Old Testament, God provided manna for the Israelites in the wilderness (Exodus 16), and in the New Testament, Jesus assures us that God knows our needs even before we ask (Matthew 6:8). This assurance of God's provision encourages us to bring our requests before Him, trusting in His generosity and care.

Jesus Christ as the Model of Prayer

Jesus Christ serves as the ultimate model for prayer. His life and ministry were marked by a deep and continuous communion with the Father, providing a perfect example for believers to follow.

The Prayer Life of Jesus

The Gospels record numerous instances of Jesus praying, often withdrawing to solitary places to spend time in prayer (Luke 5:16). Whether it was early in the morning (Mark 1:35) or during critical moments like choosing His disciples (Luke 6:12-13) and facing the cross (Matthew 26:36-46), Jesus demonstrated the importance of seeking the Father's guidance and strength through prayer.

The Lord's Prayer

One of the most significant contributions of Jesus to the theology of prayer is the Lord's Prayer (Matthew 6:9-13). This prayer encapsulates key elements of prayer: adoration, submission to God's will, petition for daily needs, confession of sins, and a plea for protection from evil. It serves as both a template and a profound theological statement on the nature of prayer.

Jesus' High Priestly Prayer

The High Priestly Prayer of Jesus is recorded in the Bible as follows:

"Father, I want those you have given me to be with me where I am, and to see my glory, the glory you have given me because you loved me before the creation of the world. Righteous Father, though the world does not know you, I know you, and they know that you have sent me. I have made you known to them, and will continue to make you known in order that the love you have for me may be in them and that I myself may be in them." **(John 17:24-26, NIV)**.

In this prayer, Jesus intercedes for His disciples and future believers. This prayer highlights Jesus' role as an intercessor and underscores the importance of praying for others. It also reflects His deep desire for unity among believers and their sanctification through the truth of God's Word.

The Role of the Holy Spirit in Prayer

The Holy Spirit plays a vital role in the prayer life of believers. As the third person of the Trinity, the Spirit empowers, guides, and intercedes for us, making our prayers effective and aligned with God's will.

The Spirit as Helper

Jesus promised His disciples that the Holy Spirit would come as a Helper (John 14:16). The Spirit assists believers in prayer, providing the strength and perseverance needed to maintain a consistent prayer life. This divine assistance ensures that even in our weakness, we can approach God with confidence.

The Spirit's Intercession

One of the profound roles of the Holy Spirit is intercession. Romans 8:26-27 reveals that the Spirit intercedes for us with "groanings too deep for words." This intercession is crucial when we are unsure how to pray or what to pray for. The Spirit aligns our prayers with God's will, ensuring that they are in accordance with His purposes.

The Spirit's Guidance

The Holy Spirit also guides believers in prayer. Ephesians 6:18 encourages us to pray "in the Spirit," suggesting a dynamic and responsive prayer life led by the Holy Spirit. This guidance helps us discern God's will and pray accordingly, enhancing the effectiveness and depth of our prayers.

The Purpose of Prayer

Understanding the purpose of prayer is essential to fully grasp its significance in the Christian life. Prayer serves several vital functions, each contributing to the spiritual growth and well-being of the believer.

Communion with God

At its heart, prayer is about communion with God. It is a means of building and nurturing a relationship with the Creator. Through prayer, we draw near to God, experience His presence, and grow in our understanding of His nature and will.

Spiritual Formation

Prayer is a tool for spiritual formation. It shapes our character, aligning our hearts and minds with God's purposes. As we spend time in prayer, we are transformed, becoming more like Christ in our thoughts, attitudes, and actions.

Intercession and Advocacy

Another key purpose of prayer is intercession. We are called to pray for others, lifting their needs before God. This act of intercession is a form of advocacy, where we stand in the gap for those who may be struggling, suffering, or in need of divine intervention.

The Power of Prayer

Prayer is not merely a passive activity; it is a powerful force that can bring about change in the spiritual and physical realms.

Transforming Lives

Prayer has the power to transform lives. Through consistent and fervent prayer, individuals experience personal breakthroughs, healing, and restoration. Testimonies abound of how prayer has led to miraculous changes in health, relationships, and circumstances.

Influencing Events

Prayer also has the power to influence events. Biblical accounts, such as Elijah's prayer for rain (1 Kings 18:41-45) and Peter's release from prison through the church's prayer (Acts 12:5-17), demonstrate how prayer can alter the course of history. Believers are called to pray with the expectation that God will move in response to their petitions.

The Communal Aspect of Prayer

Prayer is not solely an individual practice; it has a significant communal dimension that strengthens the body of Christ.

Corporate Worship

Corporate prayer is a vital component of communal worship. When believers gather to pray together, they unite their hearts and voices in seeking God's presence and guidance. This unity fosters a sense of community and shared purpose, enhancing the spiritual vitality of the church.

Collective Intercession

Collective intercession involves the church coming together to pray for specific needs, whether they are local, national, or global. This unified approach amplifies the power of prayer, demonstrating the strength of the church's collective faith and commitment to God's mission.

Conclusion

The theology of prayer is rich and multifaceted, grounded in the character of God, exemplified by Jesus Christ, and empowered by the Holy Spirit. Understanding these theological foundations transforms our approach to prayer, making it a profound and dynamic encounter with the divine. As we grow in our knowledge of God's character, follow the example of Jesus, and rely on the Holy Spirit, our prayer lives become more vibrant and impactful, drawing us closer to God and aligning us with His purposes. Prayer serves as a powerful tool for personal transformation, spiritual formation, and communal unity, ultimately leading to a deeper and more effective Christian witness in the world.

Closing Prayer

Heavenly Father,

We thank You for the journey we have taken through this chapter on the theology of prayer. Thank You for opening our minds and hearts to the profound truths and divine mysteries that underpin our communication with You. We are grateful for the depth of understanding You have imparted to us about the nature and purpose of prayer.

Lord, as we conclude this chapter, we ask that You deepen our conviction and enrich our practice of prayer. Help us to grasp the theological foundations we have explored and to integrate these truths into our daily lives. May our prayers be grounded in a sound understanding of who You are, Your will, and Your purposes for us.

Strengthen our faith, Lord, so that we may approach You with confidence and trust, knowing that You are a loving and sovereign God who hears and answers our prayers. Teach us to pray with hearts full of reverence, humility, and love, always seeking to align our desires with Your divine will.

We ask that You continue to guide us, shaping our prayer lives to reflect Your character and glory. May our prayers be a means of drawing closer to You, deepening our relationship with You, and participating in Your work in the world.

Thank You, Lord, for the gift of prayer and for the rich theological insights You have given us. May we carry these truths with us, allowing them to transform our hearts and our lives.

In the precious name of Jesus Christ, our Lord and Saviour, we pray.

Amen.

CHAPTER 4

PRAYER IN THE LIFE OF THE BELIEVER

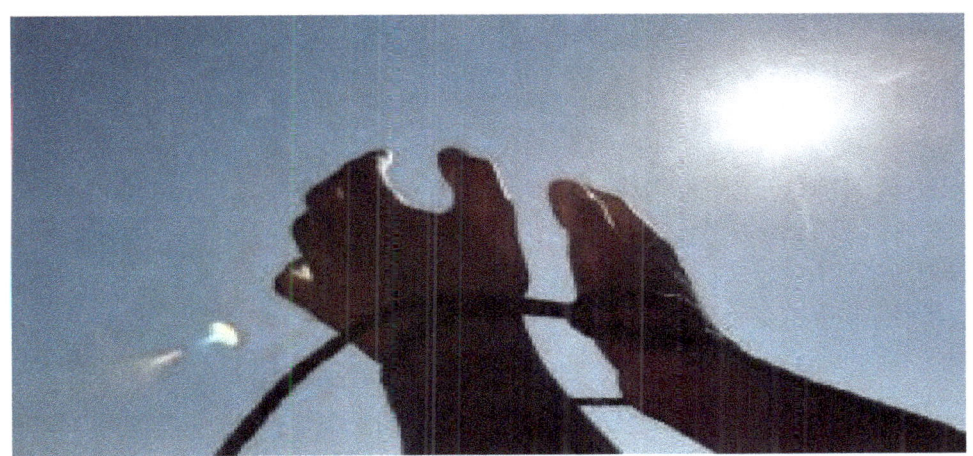

Prayer can set you free.

Opening Prayer

Heavenly Father,

As we begin this chapter on "Prayer in the Life of the Believer," we come before You with gratitude and anticipation. Thank You for the gift of prayer, through which we can communicate with You, find solace, and seek guidance. We are eager to explore how prayer can shape and enrich our daily walk with You.

Lord, we ask for Your wisdom and insight as we delve into the significance of prayer in the life of a believer. Open our hearts and minds to understand the vital role prayer plays in our spiritual growth, our relationship with You, and our ability to live out our faith. May we be inspired to deepen our commitment to a life of prayer.

Holy Spirit, be our guide and teacher in this journey. Illuminate the truths we will discover in this chapter and help us to apply them to our lives. Show us the transformative power of consistent and heartfelt prayer, and how it aligns us with Your will and purpose.

Remove any distractions or doubts that may hinder our understanding and practice of prayer. Fill us with a desire to seek You earnestly and to make prayer a central part of our daily lives. May our time in this chapter draw us closer to You and strengthen our faith.

Lord, as we explore "Prayer in the Life of the Believer," may we be encouraged and equipped to build a vibrant and dynamic prayer life. Let our prayers be a reflection of our trust in You, our love for You, and our dependence on Your grace.

In the precious name of Jesus Christ, our Lord and Saviour, we pray.

Amen.

Introduction

In the previous chapter, we focused on the theology of prayer, emphasizing the character of God and prayer, Christ as the model of prayer, and the role of the Holy Spirit in prayer. In this chapter, our emphasis is on the role that prayer plays in the life of the believer. Specifically, we explore the following themes: personal relationship with God, daily devotion and prayer life, and the transformative power of prayer.

Personal Relationship with God

Prayer is the cornerstone of a believer's personal relationship with God. It is through prayer that we communicate with our Creator, sharing our thoughts, fears, joys, and sorrows. This intimate dialogue is not merely a ritual but a profound expression of our faith and trust in God. When we pray, we open our hearts to God's presence, allowing Him to work within us and guide us. This relationship is nurtured by honesty, humility, and a genuine desire to draw closer to God.

Through prayer, we come to understand God's will for our lives. It is in these quiet moments of reflection and conversation that we can seek His guidance and wisdom. As we develop this relationship, we learn to listen to His voice, discern His plans, and find comfort in His promises. The deeper our relationship with God, the more we can experience His love and grace in our daily lives.

Daily Devotion and Prayer Life

A vibrant prayer life requires consistency and dedication. Daily devotion is a discipline that helps believers stay connected to God amidst the busyness of life. Setting aside specific times each day for prayer and reflection creates a rhythm that prioritizes our spiritual well-being.

Morning prayers can set the tone for the day, inviting God's presence and guidance into our activities. Evening prayers offer a time for reflection, gratitude, and seeking forgiveness for any shortcomings. Additionally, incorporating scripture reading into our daily devotion enriches our understanding of God's word and His character. By immersing ourselves in the Bible, we find inspiration and strength to face life's challenges.

Maintaining a prayer journal can also be a valuable practice. Writing down prayers, reflections, and insights allows us to track our spiritual growth and see how God answers our prayers over time. It is a tangible way to witness God's faithfulness and His involvement in our lives.

The Transformative Power of Prayer

Prayer has the power to transform not only our circumstances but also our hearts and minds. When we pray, we invite God's transformative work within us, aligning our desires with His will. This transformation is often gradual, as prayer shapes our character, attitudes, and perspectives.

One of the most profound ways prayer transforms us is by fostering a spirit of humility and dependence on God. In acknowledging our limitations and surrendering our burdens to Him, we become more aware of His sovereignty and grace. This humility allows us to grow in faith and trust, knowing that God is fully in control.

Prayer also cultivates a sense of peace and contentment. In times of anxiety and uncertainty, prayer can calm our hearts and remind us of God's promises. As we cast our cares upon Him, we experience a peace that surpasses all understanding, guarding our hearts and minds in Christ Jesus (Philippians 4:7).

Moreover, prayer empowers us to love and forgive others. As we pray for those who have wronged us, God softens our hearts and helps us extend grace and mercy. This process of forgiveness is liberating, freeing us from bitterness and resentment.

Corporate Prayer and Community

While personal prayer is essential, corporate prayer plays a significant role in the life of the believer. Gathering with other believers to pray strengthens the bonds of Christian fellowship and unity. In the early church, believers devoted themselves to prayer together, experiencing the power of collective intercession (Acts 2:42).

Corporate prayer provides an opportunity to support and encourage one another. Praying with others allows us to share our burdens, celebrate our victories, and seek God's guidance as a community of faith. It is a reminder that we are not alone in our spiritual journey but are part of a larger body of Christ.

Additionally, corporate prayer can be a powerful witness to the world. When believers unite in prayer, it demonstrates the unity and love that Christ desires for His followers. It can also be a source of hope and inspiration for those who are seeking or struggling in their faith.

Intercessory Prayer

Intercessory prayer is the act of praying on behalf of others. It is a selfless expression of love and concern, as we bring the needs of our friends, family, and even strangers before God. The Bible encourages us to intercede for others, following the example of Jesus, who intercedes for us at the right hand of the Father (Romans 8:34).

Intercessory prayer can have a profound impact on the lives of those we pray for. It is an opportunity to stand in the gap and seek God's intervention in their situations. Whether we are praying for healing, provision, or spiritual awakening, intercessory prayer allows us to partner with God in His work in the world.

Furthermore, intercessory prayer can deepen our compassion and empathy. As we pray for others, we become more aware of their struggles and needs, prompting us to act in love and service. It also strengthens our faith as we witness God's responses to our prayers.

The following is an example of an intercessory prayer of a mother on behalf of her children.

Heavenly Father,

I come before You with a heavy heart, burdened by the choices and struggles of my children who have strayed from Your path. As their mother, I love them deeply and long to see them walk in Your ways, experiencing the peace, joy, and purpose that only You can give.

Lord, I lift up my children, Mark. Victoria, and Samuel to You, asking for Your divine intervention in their lives. You know their hearts and the paths they have taken. Reach out to them with Your boundless love and mercy, drawing them back to You. Surround them with Your presence, even in their rebellion and confusion, and remind them of Your unfailing love.

I pray, Father, that the Holy Spirit will convict their hearts and open their eyes to the truth. Remove any blinders that keep them from seeing Your light. Break the chains of any influences or habits that have led them astray. Grant them the courage to turn away from their wayward ways and seek forgiveness and restoration in You.

Lord, give me the strength and wisdom to continue loving and supporting my children, even when it's difficult. Help me to be a reflection of Your love and grace, offering guidance without judgment and hope without despair. Grant me patience to trust in Your timing and to remain steadfast in prayer.

I pray for protection over my children, shielding them from harm and guiding them safely back to Your embrace. Place godly influences and mentors in their lives who can speak truth and encouragement to them. Let Your Word penetrate their hearts and minds, bringing clarity and a renewed sense of purpose.

Father, I know that You are a God of miracles, and nothing is impossible for You. I place my children Mark, Victoria, and Samuel in Your capable hands, trusting that You will work all things for their good and Your glory. Strengthen my faith as I wait for their return to You, and grant me peace in the midst of uncertainty.

Thank You for hearing my prayers and for Your promise to never leave us nor forsake us. I surrender my children to You, confident in Your power to transform their lives. May Your will be done in their lives, and may they come to know and love You deeply.

In the precious name of Jesus, our Saviour and Redeemer, I pray.

Amen.

Listening Prayer

Prayer is not only about speaking to God but also about listening to Him. Listening prayer involves quieting our hearts and minds to hear God's voice. This practice requires patience and attentiveness, as we seek to discern His guidance and direction.

Listening prayer can be facilitated through practices such as meditation, silence, and contemplative reading of scripture. By creating space for God to speak, we become more attuned to His presence and leading in our lives.

God speaks to us in various ways—through His word, through the Holy Spirit, and through the counsel of others. Developing a listening posture in prayer helps us recognize and respond to His voice, leading to greater intimacy and alignment with His will.

Prayer and Spiritual Warfare

Prayer is a vital weapon in the believer's arsenal for spiritual warfare. Ephesians 6:12 reminds us that our struggle is not against flesh and blood but against spiritual forces of evil. In this battle, prayer is our means of accessing God's power and protection.

Through prayer, we can resist the enemy's attacks, claim God's promises, and stand firm in our faith. It is important to be vigilant and persistent in prayer, seeking God's strength and wisdom to overcome the challenges we face.

Praying the scriptures is a powerful way to engage in spiritual warfare. By declaring God's truth and promises, we can counter the lies and deceptions of the enemy. Additionally, praying in the Spirit, as described in Ephesians 6:18, allows us to pray according to God's will and in alignment with His purposes.

Conclusion

Prayer is an indispensable part of the believer's life, shaping our relationship with God, guiding our daily walk, transforming our hearts, and empowering us for service and spiritual warfare. As we cultivate a rich and consistent prayer life, we experience the fullness of God's presence, power, and purpose in our lives. Through prayer, we draw closer to God, grow in faith, and become vessels of His love and grace in the world.

Closing Prayer

Gracious and Loving Father,

Thank You for the wisdom, insights, and encouragement You have provided us through these pages. We are reminded of the vital role that prayer plays in our daily walk with You, and we are deeply thankful for this divine gift that draws us closer to Your heart.

Lord, we ask that You take the truths we have learned and plant them firmly in our hearts. Help us to cultivate a vibrant and consistent prayer life, one that reflects our dependence on You and our desire to know You more intimately. Teach us to pray with faith, sincerity, and persistence, trusting in Your goodness and Your perfect timing.

As we navigate the journey of life, may prayer be our constant companion, our source of strength, and our refuge in times of need. Guide us to be mindful of Your presence in every moment, lifting our hearts to You in praise, thanksgiving, and supplication. Let our prayers be an expression of our love for You and our commitment to Your will.

Father, empower us to be not only hearers of Your Word but doers also. May our prayer lives bear fruit in our actions, reflecting Your love, grace, and truth to those around us. Strengthen our resolve to intercede for others, to seek Your guidance in all things, and to remain steadfast in our faith.

We thank You for Your faithfulness, Your mercy, and Your unending love. As we move forward, may our lives be a testament to the power of prayer and the transformative relationship we have with You.

In the name of Jesus Christ, our Lord and Saviour, we pray.

Amen.

CHAPTER 5
PRAYER WITH FAITH

Pray with Faith and He will answer.

Opening Prayer

Heavenly Father,

We come before You with hearts eager to learn and grow in our understanding of praying with faith. Open our minds to comprehend Your Word and open our hearts to receive Your truth. Strengthen our faith as we seek to draw closer to You through prayer. May this chapter be a source of inspiration and encouragement, leading us to trust You more deeply and pray with unwavering faith. In Jesus' name, we pray.

Amen.

Introduction

Praying with faith is a cornerstone of the Christian life, encompassing a deep trust in God's promises and His power to fulfil them. Faith transforms our prayers from mere words into powerful declarations that align with God's will. As Hebrews 11:1 states, "Now faith is the assurance of things hoped for, the conviction of things not seen." This chapter delves into what it means to pray with faith, exploring biblical examples, practical steps, and the profound impact faith-filled prayers can have on our lives and the lives of others.

The Essence of Praying with Faith

What is Faith?

Faith, in its simplest form, is trust and confidence in God. It is believing in His character, His promises, and His power. As the author of Hebrews emphasizes:

"And without faith it is impossible to please him, for whoever would draw near to God must believe that he exists and that he rewards those who seek him." **(Hebrews 11:6)**.

Biblical Foundations

The Bible is replete with examples of faith-filled prayers. The following are examples:

Abraham's prayer for a son

But Abram said, "Sovereign LORD, what can you give me since I remain childless and the one who will inherit my estate is Eliezer of Damascus?" And Abram said, "You have given me no children; so a servant in my household will be my heir."

Then the word of the LORD came to him: "This man will not be your heir, but a son who is your own flesh and blood will be your heir." He took him outside and said, *"Look up at the sky and count the stars—if indeed you can count them." Then he said to him, "So shall your offspring be."*

Abram believed the LORD, *and he credited it to him as righteousness.* **(Genesis 15:2-6, NIV).**

Moses' intercession for the Israelites

But Moses sought the favor of the LORD *his God. "*LORD,*" he said, "why should your anger burn against your people, whom you brought out of Egypt with great power and a mighty hand? Why should the Egyptians say, 'It was with evil intent that he brought them out, to kill them in the mountains and to wipe them off the face of the earth'? Turn from your fierce anger; relent and do not bring disaster on your people. Remember your servants Abraham, Isaac and Israel, to whom you swore by your own self: 'I will make your descendants as numerous as the stars in the sky and I will give your descendants all this land I promised them, and it will be their inheritance forever.'" Then the* LORD *relented and did not bring on his people the disaster he had threatened.* **(Exodus 32:11-14, NIV).**

Elijah's prayer for rain

And Elijah said to Ahab, "Go, eat and drink, for there is the sound of a heavy rain." So Ahab went off to eat and drink, but Elijah climbed to the top of Carmel, bent down to the ground and put his face between his knees. "Go and look toward the sea," he told his servant. And he went up and looked. "There is nothing there," he said. Seven times Elijah said, "Go back." The seventh time the servant reported, "A cloud as small as a man's hand is rising from the sea." So Elijah said, "Go and tell Ahab, 'Hitch up your chariot and go down before the rain stops you.'" Meanwhile, the sky grew black with clouds, the wind rose, a heavy rain started falling and Ahab rode off to Jezreel. **(1Kings 18:41-45, NIV).**

Jesus Himself often highlighted the importance of faith in prayer, saying in Matthew 21:22,

"And whatever you ask in prayer, you will receive, if you have faith."

Practical Steps to Praying with Faith

Know God's Promises

To pray with faith, it is essential to know God's promises as revealed in Scripture. Familiarize yourself with verses that speak to God's faithfulness, provision, healing, and guidance. By aligning your prayers with His promises, you can pray with greater confidence.

Cultivate a Relationship with God

Faith grows through a personal relationship with God. Spend time in His presence through prayer, worship, and reading the Bible. As you get to know God more intimately, your trust in Him will deepen, enhancing your ability to pray with faith.

Speak in Alignment with God's Word

Faith-filled prayers often involve declaring God's Word over situations. Speak Scriptures that align with your prayers, believing that God's Word is powerful and active. For instance, when praying for peace, declare Philippians 4:6-7 over your life.

"Do not be anxious about anything, but in every situation, by prayer and petition, with thanksgiving, present your requests to God. And the peace of God, which transcends all understanding, will guard your hearts and your minds in Christ Jesus."

Practice Patience and Persistence

Praying with faith requires patience and persistence. Sometimes, answers to prayers are not immediate. Trust in God's timing and continue to pray with steadfast faith, as Jesus taught in the parable of the persistent widow (Luke 18:1-8).

Then Jesus told his disciples a parable to show them that they should always pray and not give up. He said: "In a certain town there was a judge who neither feared

God nor cared what people thought. And there was a widow in that town who kept coming to him with the plea, 'Grant me justice against my adversary.'

"For some time he refused. But finally he said to himself, 'Even though I don't fear God or care what people think, yet because this widow keeps bothering me, I will see that she gets justice, so that she won't eventually come and attack me!'"

And the Lord said, "Listen to what the unjust judge says. And will not God bring about justice for his chosen ones, who cry out to him day and night? Will he keep putting them off? I tell you, he will see that they get justice, and quickly. However, when the Son of Man comes, will he find faith on the earth?" **(Luke 18:1-8, NIV)**.

Overcome Doubt

Doubt can undermine faith. Combat doubt by focusing on God's past faithfulness and the testimonies of others. Remember James warns against praying with a doubting heart.

But when you ask, you must believe and not doubt, because the one who doubts is like a wave of the sea, blown and tossed by the wind. That person should not expect to receive anything from the Lord. **(James 1:6-7, NIV)**.

Seek to cultivate a mindset of unwavering trust in God.

The Impact of Faith-Filled Prayers

Personal Transformation

Praying with faith transforms us personally. It builds our trust in God, strengthens our relationship with Him, and brings inner peace and confidence. Faith-filled prayers align our hearts with God's will, allowing us to experience His presence and power more fully.

Influencing Others

When we pray with faith, it can have a profound impact on those around us. Our prayers can bring healing, provision, and breakthroughs in the lives of others. Faith-filled prayers can also inspire and encourage fellow believers, fostering a community of strong faith.

Witnessing God's Power

Praying with faith allows us to witness God's miraculous power. As we trust Him for the impossible, we open the door for His supernatural intervention. Whether it's healing the sick, restoring relationships, or providing in times of need, faith-filled prayers enable us to see God's hand at work in extraordinary ways.

Conclusion

Praying with faith is an invitation to experience the fullness of God's promises and power in our lives. It requires knowing His Word, cultivating a deep relationship with Him, and trusting in His timing and goodness. As we pray with unwavering faith, we not only transform our own lives but also become vessels of God's blessings to others. Let us embrace the call to pray with faith, confident that our prayers can move mountains and bring about God's divine will.

Closing Prayer

Gracious Father,

We thank You for the insights and truths revealed in this chapter on praying with faith. Strengthen our hearts to trust in You fully and to pray with confidence, knowing that You hear us and are faithful to Your promises. Help us to overcome doubt and to stand firm in our faith, no matter the circumstances. May our faith-filled prayers bring glory to Your name and blessings to those around us. As we continue our journey of faith, may we always seek to deepen our relationship with You and align our lives with Your will. In Jesus' powerful name, we pray.

Amen.

Word Puzzles

FOUNDATIONS OF PRAYER

CROSSWORD

Across

5 ASSOCIATE WITH PEOPLE WHO HAVE MUTUAL INTERESTS

7 AN ADMISSION OF GUILT

9 A MARKED CHANGE IN FORM, APPEARANCE OR NATURE

10 A STATE OF BEING SET FREE

11 A FEELING OF PROFOUND LOVE AND ADMIRATION

14 ON WHO INTERVENES ON BEHALF OF ANOTHER

18 THE ACT OF YIELDING TO A SUPERIOR FORCE

Down

1 PROFOUND DEDICATION TO GOD

2 GREAT TRUST AND STRONG BELIEF IN GOD

3 SOMEONE WITH RELIGIOUS FAITH

4 GUARANTEE OF SOMETHING

6 THE STATE OF BEING MADE HOLY

8 THE SHARING OF INTIMATE THOUGHTS AND FEELINGS

12 A REQUEST ASKING SOMEONE TO GRANT SOMETHING

13 COMMUNICATION WITH GOD

15 THREE IN ONE

16 RELATING TO RELIGIOUS BELIEFS

17 OF OR LIKE GOD

FOUNDATIONS OF PRAYER
CROSSWORD
ANSWER

										D			
					F					E			
					A					V			
					I					O			
		B			T					T	A		
	F	E	L	L	O	W	S	H	I	P	I	S	
		L			A					I	S		
		I		C	O	N	F	E	S	S	I	O	N	U
		E			C						R		C
		V		T	R	A	N	S	F	O	R	M	A	T	I	O	N
		E			I						N		M
		R			V						C		M
				D	E	L	I	V	E	R	A	N	C	E	E		U
					C								N
					A	D	O	R	A	T	I	O	N	I
		P			T						P		O
		E			I	N	T	E	R	S	E	S	S	O	R	N
		T		D		C		R			P		A
S	U	B	M	I	S	S	I	O	N		I		Y
		T		V				I			R		E
		I		I				N			I		R
		O		N				I			T	
		N		E				T			U	
								Y			A	
											L	

Across

5 ASSOCIATE WITH PEOPLE WHO HAVE MUTUAL INTERESTS
7 AN ADMISSION OF GUILT
9 A MARKED CHANGE IN FORM, APPEARANCE OR NATURE
10 A STATE OF BEING SET FREE
11 A FEELING OF PROFOUND LOVE AND ADMIRATION
14 ON WHO INTERVENES ON BEHALF OF ANOTHER
18 THE ACT OF YIELDING TO A SUPERIOR FORCE

Down

1 PROFOUND DEDICATION TO GOD
2 GREAT TRUST AND STRONG BELIEF IN GOD
3 SOMEONE WITH RELIGIOUS FAITH
4 GUARANTEE OF SOMETHING
6 THE STATE OF BEING MADE HOLY
8 THE SHARING OF INTIMATE THOUGHS AND FEELINGS
12 A REQUEST ASKING SOMEONE TO GRANT SOMETHING
13 COMMUNICATION WITH GOD
15 THREE IN ONE
16 RELATING TO RELIGIOUS BELIEFS
17 OF OR LIKE GOD

FOUNDATIONS OF PRAYER
WORDSEARCH

```
S P P G N A I T S I R H C
E S P I R I T F X L J E U
L A D O R A T I O N C D D
T D H G A R M W N O D E E
S I U O I S B N N I L C N
O A M N L L S F X I P R I
P R I B E Y E U V B L E V
A T E S U S Q E R L F T I
Y E S Y S S R F G A M N D
V E M I A A F C W G N I D
D K O U N R V S M I I C C
N N B C L T P D G C H Y E
F E E N O P E T I T I O N
```

ADORATION	CONFESSION	PETITION
APOSTLES	DELIVERANCE	PRAYER
ASSURANCE	DIVINE	SPIRIT
BLESSED	HOLY	SUBMIT
CHRISTIAN	INTERCEDE	TRINITY

FOUNDATIONS OF PRAYER
WORDSEARCH--ANSWER

	1	2	3	4	5	6	7	8	9	10	11	12	13
1	S	P	P	G	N	A	I	T	S	I	R	H	C
2	E	S	P	I	R	I	T	F	X	L	J	E	U
3	L	A	D	O	R	A	T	I	O	N	C	D	D
4	T	D	H	G	A	R	M	W	N	O	D	E	E
5	S	I	U	O	I	S	B	N	N	I	L	C	N
6	O	A	M	N	L	L	S	F	X	I	P	R	I
7	P	R	I	B	E	Y	E	U	V	B	L	E	V
8	A	T	E	S	U	S	Q	E	R	L	F	T	I
9	Y	E	S	Y	S	S	R	F	G	A	M	N	D
10	V	E	M	I	A	A	F	C	W	G	N	I	D
11	D	K	O	U	N	R	V	S	M	I	I	C	C
12	N	N	B	C	L	T	P	D	G	C	H	Y	E
13	F	B	E	N	O	P	E	T	I	T	I	O	N

The words below are listed with their starting row and column

ADORATION 3:2	CONFESSION 3:11	PETITION 13:6
APOSTLES 8:1	DELIVERANCE 3:13	PRAYER 12:7
ASSURANCE 4:5	DIVINE 9:13	SPIRIT 2:2
BLESSED 5:7	HOLY 4:3	SUBMIT 9:6
CHRISTIAN 1:13	INTERCEDE 10:12	TRINITY 3:7

PART II

TYPES AND FORMS OF PRAYER

CHAPTER 6

ADORATION AND WORSHIP

The heavens declare the glory of God.

Opening Prayer

Heavenly Father,

As we begin this chapter on "Adoration and Worship," we come before You with hearts full of awe and reverence. You are the Creator of the heavens and the earth, the King of kings, and the Lord of lords. We acknowledge Your greatness, Your majesty, and Your infinite love. We are humbled by Your presence and grateful for the privilege of worshiping You.

Lord, we ask for Your guidance and inspiration as we delve into the beauty and depth of adoration and worship. Open our hearts and minds to fully comprehend what it means to adore You, to lift up Your name, and to honour You with our whole being. Teach us to worship You in spirit and in truth, with sincere hearts and undivided attention.

Let Your Holy Spirit fill us with a fresh awareness of Your glory and holiness. Illuminate the scriptures and truths we will explore in this chapter, and draw us closer to the heart of the Father. May our study lead us into deeper expressions of adoration, where our lives become a continuous offering of praise and thanksgiving.

Remove any distractions or hindrances that prevent us from fully engaging in worship. Help us to lay aside our worries, our fears, and our doubts, and to focus solely on You. Let our worship be a sweet aroma, pleasing to You, as we declare Your goodness and proclaim Your mighty works.

Lord, we desire to know You more and to experience the fullness of Your presence. As we embark on this journey of understanding adoration and worship, may our hearts be transformed and our relationship with You be enriched. Let our lives be a testament to Your glory, and may our worship bring honour to Your name.

In the precious name of Jesus Christ, our Lord and Saviour, we pray.

Amen.

Introduction

Adoration and worship are fundamental aspects of the believer's relationship with God. They go beyond mere rituals and traditions, representing the heart's deep reverence and love for the Creator. Adoration involves honouring God for who He is, while worship encompasses our expressions of devotion, praise, and gratitude. Together, they form the foundation of a vibrant spiritual life, drawing us closer to God's presence and transforming our hearts. This chapter deals with praising God for who He is, scriptural examples of worshipful prayer, incorporating worship into daily prayer, and the role of the Holy Spirit in worship.

Praising God for Who He Is

Adoration begins with acknowledging the attributes and character of God. It is an act of praising God not just for what He has done but for who He is. Recognizing His holiness, love, mercy, justice, amazing grace, and sovereignty leads us to a place of awe and reverence. This form of praise is not dependent on our circumstances but is rooted in the unchanging nature of God.

When we praise God for His attributes, we shift our focus from our needs and concerns to His greatness and majesty. This shift in perspective helps us cultivate a deeper sense of trust and confidence in Him. As we declare His goodness, faithfulness, and power, our faith is strengthened, and our spirits are uplifted.

Scriptural Examples of Worshipful Prayer

The Bible is replete with examples of worshipful prayer that highlight the essence of adoration. These prayers serve as models for us to follow, guiding us in expressing our love and reverence for God.

David's Psalms

Many of David's psalms are beautiful expressions of worship and adoration. Psalm 145, for instance, is a profound declaration of God's greatness and His mighty acts. David's heartfelt prayers reflect his deep love for God and his desire to exalt Him above all else.

Hannah's Prayer

In 1 Samuel 2:1-10, Hannah's prayer of thanksgiving and worship is a powerful example of adoration. After God answers her plea for a child, she responds with a prayer that exalts God's holiness, knowledge, and sovereignty.

Mary's Magnificat

In Luke 1:46-55, Mary's song of praise, known as the Magnificat, is a beautiful expression of worship. She glorifies God for His mercy, strength, and faithfulness, recognizing His hand in her life and in the history of His people.

The Lord's Prayer

Jesus' model prayer in Matthew 6:9-13 begins with an acknowledgment of God's holiness and sovereignty: "Our Father in heaven, hallowed be Your name." This opening phrase sets the tone for adoration, emphasizing the importance of honouring God's name in our prayers.

Incorporating Worship into Daily Prayer

Incorporating worship into our daily prayer life involves intentional practices that draw our hearts into a posture of adoration. Here are some practical ways to weave worship into our daily routines:

Begin with Praise: Start your prayer time by praising God for His attributes. Reflect on His goodness, faithfulness, and love. Use scripture to guide your praise, declaring verses that speak of His greatness.

Sing Songs of Worship: Music is a powerful tool for worship. Singing hymns, psalms, and contemporary worship songs can help us express our adoration and connect deeply with God's presence. Make it a habit to include worship songs in your daily prayer time.

Use a Prayer Journal: Write down prayers of adoration and praise in a journal. Record the attributes of God that stand out to you and reflect on how you have seen His hand in your life. This practice helps to cultivate a heart of gratitude and reverence.

Meditate on Scripture: Spend time meditating on passages that highlight God's character and deeds. Let these scriptures shape your prayers, allowing the Word of God to inspire and guide your worship.

Express Gratitude: Incorporate thanksgiving into your prayers, acknowledging God's blessings and provisions. Gratitude naturally leads to adoration, as we recognize God's goodness in our lives.

The Role of the Holy Spirit in Worship

The Holy Spirit plays a crucial role in our worship, guiding and empowering us to worship God in spirit and truth (John 4:24). The Spirit helps us to connect with God on a deeper level, moving our hearts and aligning our desires with His.

Spirit-Led Worship

Allow the Holy Spirit to lead your worship. Be open to His prompting and guidance, whether it is through a song, a scripture, or a spontaneous prayer. The Spirit can bring to mind specific attributes of God that He wants you to focus on in your adoration.

Praying in the Spirit

Praying in tongues or allowing the Spirit to intercede through you can enhance your worship experience. This form of prayer bypasses the limitations of language and connects you directly with God's heart.

Sensitivity to the Spirit

Cultivate a sensitivity to the Holy Spirit's presence and movement during worship. This sensitivity helps you to stay attuned to God's leading and to respond in ways that honour and glorify Him.

Conclusion

Adoration and worship are vital components of a believer's spiritual life. They draw us closer to God, transform our hearts, and deepen our relationship with Him. By praising God for who He is, following scriptural examples of worshipful prayer, and incorporating worship into our daily routines, we cultivate a heart of reverence and love for our Creator. With the guidance and empowerment of the Holy Spirit, our worship becomes a powerful expression of our faith and devotion, honouring God and reflecting His glory in our lives.

Closing Prayer

Most kind and ever-loving Father,

We come before You in awe and reverence as we conclude this chapter on "Adoration and Worship." Thank You for revealing to us the beauty and significance of adoring and worshiping You. We are grateful for the moments we have spent reflecting on Your majesty, goodness, and love.

Lord, we ask that You deepen our understanding and practice of adoration and worship. Help us to see beyond our daily routines and recognize Your presence in every aspect of our lives. Teach us to worship You in spirit and in truth, offering our hearts, minds, and souls in genuine devotion.

May our adoration be a fragrant offering to You, expressing our love, gratitude, and awe. Let our worship be a reflection of our lives surrendered to Your will, honoring You in all we do. Transform our hearts so that every thought, word, and action is an act of worship, glorifying Your holy name.

Guide us to make worship a central part of our daily lives, not confined to specific times or places but woven into the very fabric of our existence. Help us to find joy and fulfillment in Your presence, and to draw strength and comfort from our communion with You.

We pray for a heart that continually seeks You, a spirit that is attuned to Your voice, and a life that radiates Your love. May our worship inspire others to seek You and to experience the profound joy of knowing and adoring You.

Thank You, Lord, for the privilege of worshiping You. As we go forward, may our adoration and worship deepen our relationship with You and transform us into true worshipers who reflect Your glory in this world.

In the precious name of Jesus Christ, our Lord and Savior, we pray.

Amen.

CHAPTER 7
CONFESSION AND REPENTANCE

If we confess our sins, He will forgive us.

Opening Prayer

Merciful and Gracious God,

As we begin this chapter on "Confession and Repentance," we come before You with humility and contrition, recognizing our need for Your forgiveness and grace. You are holy and righteous, and we acknowledge that we fall short of Your glory. Thank You for the opportunity to confess our sins and turn back to You, knowing that You are faithful to cleanse and restore us.

Lord, we ask for Your presence and guidance as we explore the vital practice of confession and repentance. Open our hearts to the truth of our need for Your mercy. Help us to see our sins clearly and to understand the ways in which we have strayed from Your will. Grant us the courage to confess our wrongdoings honestly and sincerely.

We pray for the Holy Spirit to work within us to bring about genuine repentance. Soften our hearts and remove any pride or resistance that hinders us from fully turning back to You. Lead us to a place of deep sorrow for our sins and a sincere desire to change. Fill us with the assurance of Your love and forgiveness, reminding us that through Jesus Christ, we are made new.

As we study and reflect on the importance of confession and repentance, let Your Word penetrate our hearts and transform our lives. May this chapter inspire us to live in a continual state of repentance, seeking Your face daily and striving to walk in Your ways.

Lord, we thank You for Your endless grace and compassion. As we journey through this chapter, may we experience the freedom and renewal that come from true repentance. Let our lives be marked by a humble and contrite spirit, always seeking to align our hearts with Yours.

In the precious name of Jesus Christ, our Lord and Saviour, we pray.

Amen.

Introduction

Confession and repentance are foundational aspects of the Christian faith, essential for maintaining a healthy relationship with God. Confession involves acknowledging our sins and shortcomings before God, while repentance signifies a genuine turning away from sin and a commitment to pursue righteousness. Together, they form a process that leads to spiritual renewal, freedom, and a deeper intimacy with God. In this chapter, we discuss the importance of confession, to whom we should confess, Biblical confession prayers, and living a life of repentance.

The Importance of Confession

Confession is vital for several reasons. First, it brings our sins into the light, where they can be addressed and forgiven. The Bible teaches that "if we confess our sins, he is faithful and just to forgive us our sins and to cleanse us from all unrighteousness" (1 John 1:9). By admitting our faults, we acknowledge our need for God's mercy and grace.

Second, confession breaks the power of secret sin. When we hide our sins, they can fester and grow, leading to guilt, shame, and separation from God. Confession, however, brings healing and restoration. James 5:16 encourages us to "confess your sins to one another and pray for one another, that you may be healed."

Finally, confession fosters humility. Admitting our wrongdoings requires us to humble ourselves before God, recognizing that we cannot achieve righteousness on our own. This humility opens the door for God's transformative work in our lives, shaping us into His image.

To Whom Should We Confess?

This question has often been debated. Here, we provide some guidance based on the Bible. Confession, a vital part of the Christian faith, is primarily directed to God. As our Creator and Redeemer, God is the ultimate authority who can forgive sins and cleanse us from all unrighteousness:

"If we confess our sins, he is faithful and just and will forgive us our sins and purify us from all unrighteousness." (1 John 1:9)

Confessing to God acknowledges His sovereignty and our dependence on His grace and mercy. This personal and direct confession allows us to be honest and transparent before Him, seeking His forgiveness and restoration.

However, the Bible also encourages believers to confess their sins to one another as part of maintaining healthy and accountable relationships within the Christian community:

"Therefore confess your sins to each other and pray for each other so that you may be healed. The prayer of a righteous person is powerful and effective." (James 5:16)

This practice of mutual confession fosters an environment of support, encouragement, and accountability. It helps to break the power of secret sin, promotes healing, and strengthens the bonds of fellowship among believers. Confessing to a trusted friend, pastor, or spiritual mentor can provide the necessary guidance and prayer support needed for spiritual growth and repentance.

Biblical Confession Prayers

The Bible provides numerous examples of confession prayers that guide us in expressing our repentance and seeking God's forgiveness. These prayers serve as models for us to follow, helping us articulate our contrition and desire for renewal.

David's Prayer of Repentance

David pours out his heart in confession after his sin with Bathsheba:

"Have mercy on me, O God, according to your unfailing love; according to your great compassion blot out my transgressions. Wash away all my iniquity and cleanse me from my sin. For I know my transgressions, and my sin is always before me. Against you, you only, have I sinned and done what is evil in your sight; so you are right in your verdict and justified when you judge. Surely I was sinful at birth, sinful from the time my mother conceived me. Yet you desired faithfulness even in

the womb; you taught me wisdom in that secret place. Cleanse me with hyssop, and I will be clean; wash me, and I will be whiter than snow. Let me hear joy and gladness; let the bones you have crushed rejoice. Hide your face from my sins and blot out all my iniquity. Create in me a pure heart, O God, and renew a steadfast spirit within me. Do not cast me from your presence or take your Holy Spirit from me. Restore to me the joy of your salvation and grant me a willing spirit, to sustain me. Then I will teach transgressors your ways, so that sinners will turn back to you. Deliver me from the guilt of bloodshed, O God, you who are God my Savior, and my tongue will sing of your righteousness. Open my lips, Lord, and my mouth will declare your praise. You do not delight in sacrifice, or I would bring it; you do not take pleasure in burnt offerings. My sacrifice, O God, is a broken spirit; a broken and contrite heart you, God, will not despise. May it please you to prosper Zion, to build up the walls of Jerusalem. Then you will delight in the sacrifices of the righteous, in burnt offerings offered whole; then bulls will be offered on your altar."
(Psalm 51)

He begins by acknowledging his sin and appealing to God's mercy: "Have mercy on me, O God, according to your unfailing love; according to your great compassion blot out my transgressions" (Psalm 51:1). David's prayer is a profound expression of repentance, seeking not only forgiveness but also a renewed heart and spirit.

Daniel's Prayer for the People

In the following prayer, the prophet confesses the sins of Israel and intercedes on their behalf.

"Lord, the great and awesome God, who keeps his covenant of love with those who love him and keep his commandments, we have sinned and done wrong. We have been wicked and have rebelled; we have turned away from your commands and laws. We have not listened to your servants the prophets, who spoke in your name to our kings, our princes and our ancestors, and to all the people of the land.

"Lord, you are righteous, but this day we are covered with shame—the people of Judah and the inhabitants of Jerusalem and all Israel, both near and far, in all the

countries where you have scattered us because of our unfaithfulness to you. We and our kings, our princes and our ancestors are covered with shame, LORD, because we have sinned against you. The Lord our God is merciful and forgiving, even though we have rebelled against him; we have not obeyed the LORD our God or kept the laws he gave us through his servants the prophets. All Israel has transgressed your law and turned away, refusing to obey you.

"Therefore the curses and sworn judgments written in the Law of Moses, the servant of God, have been poured out on us, because we have sinned against you. You have fulfilled the words spoken against us and against our rulers by bringing on us great disaster. Under the whole heaven nothing has ever been done like what has been done to Jerusalem. Just as it is written in the Law of Moses, all this disaster has come on us, yet we have not sought the favor of the LORD our God by turning from our sins and giving attention to your truth. The LORD did not hesitate to bring the disaster on us, for the LORD our God is righteous in everything he does; yet we have not obeyed him.

"Now, Lord our God, who brought your people out of Egypt with a mighty hand and who made for yourself a name that endures to this day, we have sinned, we have done wrong. Lord, in keeping with all your righteous acts, turn away your anger and your wrath from Jerusalem, your city, your holy hill. Our sins and the iniquities of our ancestors have made Jerusalem and your people an object of scorn to all those around us.

"Now, our God, hear the prayers and petitions of your servant. For your sake, Lord, look with favor on your desolate sanctuary. Give ear, our God, and hear; open your eyes and see the desolation of the city that bears your Name. We do not make requests of you because we are righteous, but because of your great mercy. Lord, listen! Lord, forgive! Lord, hear and act! For your sake, my God, do not delay, because your city and your people bear your Name." **(Daniel 9:4-14)**

Daniel admits the collective guilt of the nation and pleads for God's mercy: "We have sinned and done wrong. We have been wicked and have rebelled; we have turned away from your commands and laws."

Daniel's prayer highlights the importance of corporate confession and the need for communal repentance.

The Tax Collector's Prayer

In Luke 18:13, Jesus tells the parable of the Pharisee and the tax collector. The tax collector's simple yet profound prayer of confession is a model of humility and repentance:

"God, be merciful to me, a sinner!"

Jesus commends the tax collector's attitude, teaching that true confession comes from a humble and contrite heart.

Nehemiah's Prayer

Nehemiah's prayer is recorded in Chapter 1 of Nehemiah:

"LORD, the God of heaven, the great and awesome God, who keeps his covenant of love with those who love him and keep his commandments, let your ear be attentive and your eyes open to hear the prayer your servant is praying before you day and night for your servants, the people of Israel. I confess the sins we Israelites, including myself and my father's family, have committed against you. We have acted very wickedly toward you. We have not obeyed the commands, decrees and laws you gave your servant Moses.

"Remember the instruction you gave your servant Moses, saying, 'If you are unfaithful, I will scatter you among the nations, but if you return to me and obey my commands, then even if your exiled people are at the farthest horizon, I will gather them from there and bring them to the place I have chosen as a dwelling for my Name.

"They are your servants and your people, whom you redeemed by your great strength and your mighty hand. Lord, let your ear be attentive to the prayer of this your servant and to the prayer of your servants who delight in revering your name. Give your servant success today by granting him favor in the presence of this man."
(Nehemiah 1:5-10)

In this prayer, Nehemiah confesses the sins of Israel and seeks God's favour for the rebuilding of Jerusalem. He acknowledges the nation's disobedience and appeals to God's covenant promises: "I confess the sins we Israelites, including myself and my father's family, have committed against you" Nehemiah's prayer demonstrates the power of confession in seeking God's help and restoration.

Living a Life of Repentance

Repentance is not a one-time event but a continual process in the life of a believer. Living a life of repentance involves daily examining our hearts, turning away from sin, and seeking to align our lives with God's will.

Regular Self-Examination

Regularly examining our thoughts, actions, and motives helps us identify areas where we fall short. This self-examination should be done in light of God's word, allowing the Holy Spirit to convict us and guide us toward repentance.

Accountability: Having accountability partners—trusted fellow believers who can pray with us, challenge us, and support us—can help us stay on the path of repentance. Sharing our struggles with others provides encouragement and helps us remain committed to our spiritual growth.

Renewing the Mind: Repentance involves a transformation of the mind. The apostle Paul instructs us to "be transformed by the renewal of your mind." (Romans 12:2) This renewal comes through immersing ourselves in scripture, prayer, and the teaching of the Holy Spirit. By aligning our thoughts with God's truth, we can resist temptation and pursue righteousness.

Bearing Fruit: True repentance is evidenced by the fruit it produces in our lives. John the Baptist admonished the Pharisees to "bear fruit in keeping with repentance' (Matthew 3:8). This means that our repentance should lead to tangible changes in our behaviour, attitudes, and relationships. As we live out our repentance, we become witnesses of God's transformative power to those around us.

Conclusion

Confession and repentance are crucial components of the Christian walk. They allow us to address our sins, receive God's forgiveness, and experience His transformative grace. By following the examples of biblical confession prayers and committing to a lifestyle of repentance, we can maintain a healthy and vibrant relationship with God. As we humble ourselves, acknowledge our need for His mercy, and turn away from sin, we open our hearts to the renewing work of the Holy Spirit, leading to spiritual growth and a deeper intimacy with our Creator.

Closing Prayer

Merciful Father,

We come before You with humble hearts as we conclude this chapter on "Confession and Repentance." Thank You for guiding us through this journey of understanding the importance of acknowledging our sins and turning back to You. We are grateful for Your grace, mercy, and the promise of forgiveness through Jesus Christ.

Lord, we confess our sins before You, acknowledging the ways we have fallen short of Your glory. We repent of our wrongdoings, our selfishness, and our failures to live according to Your will. We ask for Your forgiveness, trusting in Your boundless love and compassion.

Create in us clean hearts, O God, and renew a steadfast spirit within us. Help us to truly turn away from our sins and to seek Your righteousness in all areas of our lives. Strengthen our resolve to live in obedience to Your Word and to walk in the light of Your truth.

We pray for the Holy Spirit to convict us of any hidden sins and to lead us in the path of righteousness. Grant us the courage to face our shortcomings, the humility to seek forgiveness, and the strength to make amends where needed. May our lives be a testimony of Your transformative power and grace.

Thank You, Lord, for the gift of confession and the opportunity to start anew. As we move forward, may we continually seek to live in repentance, always striving to grow closer to You and to reflect Your holiness in our lives.

We are grateful for Your unfailing love and for the redemption we have in Jesus Christ. Help us to extend the same grace and forgiveness to others, living as true ambassadors of Your love and mercy.

In the precious name of Jesus Christ, our Redeemer and Lord, we pray.

Amen.

CHAPTER 8

THANKSGIVING AND GRATITUDE

Give thanks to the Lord because He is good.

Opening Prayer

Gracious and Loving Father,

As we begin this chapter on "Thanksgiving and Gratitude," we come before You with hearts overflowing with thankfulness for Your countless blessings. You are the source of all goodness, and we are grateful for Your provision, Your love, and Your faithfulness in our lives. Thank You for the many ways You have shown Your grace and mercy to us.

Lord, we ask for Your guidance and inspiration as we delve into the practice of thanksgiving and gratitude. Open our eyes to recognize the blessings that surround us each day, and teach us to cultivate a heart of gratitude in all circumstances. Help us to see Your hand at work in our lives and to give thanks for both the big and small things.

Holy Father, we pray for Your Spirit to fill our hearts with a deep sense of appreciation and joy. Illuminate the truths we will explore in this chapter and remind us of the importance of being thankful. May our gratitude not only be expressed in our words but also in our actions, reflecting a life that is truly thankful for all that You have done and continue to do.

Remove any negativity, bitterness, or entitlement that may hinder our ability to be grateful. Instead, fill us with a spirit of thanksgiving that permeates every aspect of our lives. Help us to be mindful of Your goodness and to continually offer praise and thanks to You, no matter what we face.

Lord, as we journey through this chapter, may our hearts be transformed by a deeper understanding of thanksgiving and gratitude. Let our lives be a testament to Your goodness and may our gratitude draw us closer to You, enriching our relationship with You and with those around us.

In the precious name of Jesus Christ, our Lord and Saviour, we pray.

Amen.

Introduction

Thanksgiving and gratitude are essential elements of the Christian faith, reflecting a heart that recognizes and responds to God's blessings. These attitudes go beyond a mere response to favourable circumstances; they are expressions of faith and trust in God's goodness and sovereignty. Gratitude transforms our perspective, leading us to see God's hand in every aspect of our lives. Thanksgiving, as a form of worship, honours God and acknowledges His provision, grace, and faithfulness. In this chapter, we turn our attention to expressing thanks in prayer, stories of thanksgiving in the Bible, and cultivating an attitude of gratitude.

Expressing Thanks in Prayer

Expressing thanks in prayer is a powerful way to cultivate a grateful heart and draw closer to God. Thanksgiving prayers acknowledge God's gifts, big and small, and help us focus on His blessings rather than our challenges. Here are some practical ways to incorporate thanksgiving into our prayer life:

Start with Gratitude: Begin your prayers by thanking God for who He is and what He has done. This sets a positive tone and aligns your heart with God's goodness.

Be Specific: Thank God for specific blessings, such as health, relationships, provision, and opportunities. Recognizing particular gifts helps to deepen your appreciation.

Thank God in All Circumstances: In 1 Thessalonians 5:18, Paul encourages us to "give thanks in all circumstances." Whether in times of abundance or difficulty, expressing gratitude reminds us of God's constant presence and faithfulness.

Use Scripture: Incorporate Bible verses that express thanksgiving into your prayers. Verses like Psalm 100:4—"Enter his gates with thanksgiving, and his courts with praise!"—can guide and inspire your prayers.

Keep a Gratitude Journal: Writing down your blessings and answered prayers in a journal helps you to remember and reflect on God's faithfulness over time.

Stories of Thanksgiving in the Bible

The Bible is filled with stories of thanksgiving that highlight the importance and impact of a grateful heart. These stories provide examples for us to follow and demonstrate how gratitude honours God and transforms lives.

Hannah's Thanksgiving

The following is Hannah's prayer of thanksgiving after God :

"My heart rejoices in the LORD; in the LORD my horn is lifted high. My mouth boasts over my enemies, for I delight in your deliverance. There is no one holy like the LORD; there is no one besides you; there is no Rock like our God. Do not keep talking so proudly or let your mouth speak such arrogance, for the LORD is a God who knows, and by him deeds are weighed. The bows of the warriors are broken, but those who stumbled are armed with strength. Those who were full hire themselves out for food, but those who were hungry are hungry no more. She who was barren has borne seven children, but she who has had many sons pines away. The LORD brings death and makes alive; he brings down to the grave and raises up. The LORD sends poverty and wealth; he humbles and he exalts.

He raises the poor from the dust and lifts the needy from the ash heap; he seats them with princes and has them inherit a throne of honour. For the foundations of the earth are the LORD's; on them he has set the world. He will guard the feet of his faithful servants, but the wicked will be silenced in the place of darkness. It is not by strength that one prevails; those who oppose the LORD will be broken. The Most High will thunder from heaven; the LORD will judge the ends of the earth. He will give strength to his king and exalt the horn of his anointed." **(1 Samuel 2:1-10)**

Hannah offers a prayer of thanksgiving after God answers her plea for a child. Her prayer not only thanks God for her son, Samuel, but also exalts His holiness, power, and justice.

David's Psalms of Thanksgiving

Many of David's psalms are rich with expressions of gratitude.

Witness the following psalm:

"Praise the LORD, my soul; all my inmost being, praise his holy name. Praise the LORD, my soul, and forget not all his benefits—who forgives all your sins and heals all your diseases, who redeems your life from the pit and crowns you with love and compassion, who satisfies your desires with good things so that your youth is renewed like the eagle's. The LORD works righteousness and justice for all the oppressed. He made known his ways to Moses, his deeds to the people of Israel: The LORD is compassionate and gracious, slow to anger, abounding in love. He will not always accuse, nor will he harbor his anger forever; he does not treat us as our sins deserve or repay us according to our iniquities. For as high as the heavens are above the earth, so great is his love for those who fear him; as far as the east is from the west, so far has he removed our transgressions from us. As a father has compassion on his children, so the LORD has compassion on those who fear him; for he knows how we are formed, he remembers that we are dust. The life of mortals is like grass, they flourish like a flower of the field; the wind blows over it and it is gone, and its place remembers it no more. But from everlasting to everlasting the LORD's love is with those who fear him, and his righteousness with their children's children—with those who keep his covenant and remember to obey his precepts. The LORD has established his throne in heaven, and his kingdom rules over all. Praise the LORD, you his angels, you mighty ones who do his bidding, who obey his word. Praise the LORD, all his heavenly hosts, you his servants who do his will. Praise the LORD, all his works everywhere in his dominion. Praise the LORD, my soul." **(Psalm 103, NIV)**

David calls on his soul to "Praise the Lord, my soul, and forget not all his benefits," enumerating God's blessings, such as forgiveness, healing, and redemption.

Jesus Giving Thanks

Jesus often gave thanks to the Father. Before feeding the five thousand, He took the loaves and fish and "gave thanks" (John 6:11). At the Last Supper, He also gave thanks as He broke the bread and shared the cup, establishing a model of gratitude even in the face of impending suffering.

And he took bread, gave thanks and broke it, and gave it to them, saying, "This is my body given for you; do this in remembrance of me."

In the same way, after the supper he took the cup, saying, "This cup is the new covenant in my blood, which is poured out for you." **(Luke 22:19-20)**.

Paul's Letters

The apostle Paul frequently expressed gratitude in his epistles, often thanking God for the faith and love of the believers to whom he was writing. For example, to the Philippians, he wrote:

"I thank my God every time I remember you. In all my prayers for all of you, I always pray with joy because of your partnership in the gospel from the first day until now." **(Philippians 1:3-5)**.

Cultivating an Attitude of Gratitude

Cultivating an attitude of gratitude requires intentional practice and a shift in perspective. It involves recognizing God's hand in every situation and responding with thankfulness. Here are some practical steps to develop a grateful heart:

Practice Mindfulness: Pay attention to the blessings in your life, both big and small. Take time each day to reflect on what you are grateful for and acknowledge God's provision and grace.

Express Gratitude Regularly: Make it a habit to express thanks to God and to others. Verbalizing your gratitude reinforces it and encourages those around you.

Focus on the Positive: Train your mind to focus on the positive aspects of your life rather than dwelling on the negatives. Philippians 4:8 encourages us to think about things that are true, honourable, just, pure, lovely, and commendable.

Serve Others: Serving others helps shift your focus from your own needs to the needs of others, fostering a sense of gratitude for the ability to help and the blessings you have.

Celebrate Small Wins: Recognize and celebrate small victories and blessings. This practice helps build a habit of gratitude and highlights the many ways God works in your life.

Pray for a Grateful Heart: Ask God to help you develop a grateful heart. Prayer invites the Holy Spirit to work in you, transforming your perspective and increasing your awareness of God's blessings.

Conclusion

Thanksgiving and gratitude are powerful spiritual practices that draw us closer to God and transform our lives. By expressing thanks in prayer, reflecting on biblical examples of thanksgiving, and intentionally cultivating an attitude of gratitude, we honour God and acknowledge His goodness. Gratitude shifts our focus from our challenges to God's blessings, fostering a spirit of joy and contentment. As we practice thanksgiving, we grow in faith and trust, experiencing the fullness of God's presence and provision in our lives.

Closing Prayer

Gracious and Loving Father,

As we conclude this chapter on "Thanksgiving and Gratitude," we come before You with hearts overflowing with thanks. We are deeply grateful for Your endless blessings, Your steadfast love, and Your unchanging faithfulness. Thank You for the countless ways You provide for us, guide us, and sustain us each day.

Lord, we ask that You help us carry the lessons of thanksgiving and gratitude into our daily lives. May our hearts remain continually aware of Your goodness and our lips ever ready to offer praise and thanks. Teach us to see Your hand at work in every situation, to recognize Your grace in both the big and small moments, and to cultivate a spirit of gratitude in all circumstances.

Holy Spirit, remind us to express our gratitude not only in words but also through our actions. Let our lives reflect a deep and abiding thankfulness that draws others to You. Grant us the grace to be grateful even in challenging times, knowing that You are always with us and that Your plans for us are good.

Lord, as we move forward, may the practice of thanksgiving and gratitude transform our hearts and minds. Let it bring us closer to You and deepen our trust in Your perfect provision. May we become beacons of Your light, spreading joy and hope through our grateful hearts.

Thank You for this time of reflection and learning. May the seeds of gratitude planted in this chapter grow and flourish, enriching our relationship with You and with those around us. We offer You all our thanks and praise, now and forever.

In the precious name of Jesus Christ, our Lord and Savior, we pray.

Amen.

CHAPTER 9
SUPPLICATION AND INTERCESSION

If you ask in Jesus' name, you will receive.

Opening Prayer

Gracious and Merciful Father,

As we begin this chapter on "Supplication and Intercession," we come before You with humble hearts, eager to learn and grow in our prayer lives. We thank You for the privilege of coming into Your presence, bringing our needs and the needs of others before Your throne of grace.

Lord, we ask for Your guidance and wisdom as we explore the depths of supplication and intercession. Open our hearts and minds to understand the power and importance of these forms of prayer. Help us to grasp the significance of lifting up our own requests to You in supplication, and the profound impact of interceding on behalf of others.

Father God, allow Your Holy Spirit to be our teacher and guide throughout this chapter. Illuminate the scriptures and examples that demonstrate the effectiveness of supplication and intercession. Inspire us with stories of faithful believers who have seen Your hand move mightily in response to their prayers.

As we study and reflect, Lord, cultivate within us a heart of compassion and empathy. Teach us to pray with earnestness and faith, trusting that You hear our cries and respond according to Your perfect will. Remove any barriers of doubt or discouragement that may hinder our prayers, and fill us with a renewed passion for interceding on behalf of others.

Father, help us to see the world through Your eyes, recognizing the needs around us and responding with prayerful urgency. May our supplications and intercessions be marked by sincerity, humility, and a deep sense of partnership with You in Your redemptive work.

Thank You for the incredible privilege of being able to bring our requests and the needs of others before You. As we journey through this chapter, may we be equipped and inspired to become fervent and faithful in our prayers of supplication and intercession.

In the mighty name of Jesus Christ, our Lord and Savior, we pray.

Amen.Father

Introduction

Supplication and intercession are vital aspects of the Christian prayer life, reflecting our dependence on God and our love for others. Supplication involves earnestly presenting our needs and desires before God, trusting Him to provide according to His will. Intercession, on the other hand, is the act of praying on behalf of others, standing in the gap, and seeking God's intervention in their lives. Together, these forms of prayer deepen our relationship with God, enhance our spiritual growth, and foster a sense of community within the body of Christ. The following topics are discussed in this chapter: asking and receiving, intercessory prayer, and scriptural examples of supplication.

Asking and Receiving

Supplication is about asking God for our needs and the desires of our hearts. Jesus encourages us to bring our requests before God with faith and persistence. He says:

"Ask, and it will be given to you; seek, and you will find; knock, and it will be opened to you. For everyone who asks receives, and the one who seeks finds, and to the one who knocks it will be opened." **(Matthew 7:7-8)**.

This assurance highlights God's willingness to listen to our prayers and respond according to His perfect wisdom and timing.

The process of asking and receiving through supplication requires a heart of faith and humility. We must trust that God knows what is best for us and submit our requests to His sovereign will. James reminds us that our motives matter when we ask:

"You ask and do not receive, because you ask wrongly, to spend it on your passions." **(James 4:3)**.

Therefore, our supplications should align with God's purposes and reflect a desire for His glory and kingdom.

Effective supplication also involves persistence. Jesus taught the parable of the importunate (persistent) widow to illustrate the importance of continual prayer.

"Then Jesus told his disciples a parable to show them that they should always pray and not give up. He said: "In a certain town there was a judge who neither feared God nor cared what people thought. And there was a widow in that town who kept

coming to him with the plea, 'Grant me justice against my adversary.' "For some time he refused. But finally he said to himself, 'Even though I don't fear God or care what people think, yet because this widow keeps bothering me, I will see that she gets justice, so that she won't eventually come and attack me!'"

And the Lord said, "Listen to what the unjust judge says. And will not God bring about justice for his chosen ones, who cry out to him day and night? Will he keep putting them off? I tell you, he will see that they get justice, and quickly. However, when the Son of Man comes, will he find faith on the earth?" **(Luke 18:1-8).**

The widow's unwavering determination eventually led to justice being served, demonstrating that persistent prayer can lead to God's intervention in our lives. This persistence shows our commitment and faith in God's power to answer.

Praying for Others – Intercessory Prayer

Intercessory prayer is a profound expression of love and compassion, as we bring the needs of others before God. It reflects our understanding that we are part of a larger body, the church, and that we have a responsibility to support and uplift one another through prayer.

Intercession involves standing in the gap for others, asking God to move in their situations, whether for healing, provision, guidance, or salvation. It is an act of spiritual warfare, where we contend against the forces of darkness on behalf of others. The apostle Paul instructs us to "pray at all times in the Spirit, with all prayer and supplication. To that end, keep alert with all perseverance, making supplication for all the saints." (Ephesians 6:18).

Praying for others also helps to cultivate empathy and selflessness. As we focus on the needs of others, we become more aware of their struggles and challenges, fostering a deeper sense of community and mutual support. Additionally, intercessory prayer aligns our hearts with God's love and compassion, helping us to grow in Christlikeness.

Scriptural Examples of Supplication

The Bible provides numerous examples of supplication that illustrate the power and importance of this form of prayer. These examples serve as guides and inspiration for our own prayer lives.

Jabez's Prayer

Jabez's prayer is a classic example of a prayer of supplication.

Jabez cried out to the God of Israel, "Oh, that you would bless me and enlarge my territory! Let your hand be with me, and keep me from harm so that I will be free from pain." And God granted his request. **(1 Chronicles 4:10, NIV).**

Solomon's Prayer for Wisdom

Solomon's supplication for wisdom to govern God's people is presented below:

"Now, LORD my God, you have made your servant king in place of my father David. But I am only a little child and do not know how to carry out my duties. Your servant is here among the people you have chosen, a great people, too numerous to count or number. So give your servant a discerning heart to govern your people and to distinguish between right and wrong. For who is able to govern this great people of yours?" **(1 Kings 3:7-9, NIV).**

This prayer was pleasing to the Lord. Instead of asking for personal gain, Solomon sought what would benefit others. God granted his request and blessed him with unparalleled wisdom and understanding.

Jesus' Prayer in Gethsemane

Jesus' prayer in the Garden of Gethsemane is recorded below:

"Going a little farther, he fell with his face to the ground and prayed, "My Father, if it is possible, may this cup be taken from me. Yet not as I will, but as you will."

He went away a second time and prayed, "My Father, if it is not possible for this cup to be taken away unless I drink it, may your will be done." **(Matthew 26:39, 42, NIV).**

Jesus' supplication in the Garden of Gethsemane reveals His humanity and submission to the Father's will. Faced with immense suffering, Jesus prayed, *"My Father, if it is possible, may this cup be taken from me. Yet not as I will, but as you will."* His prayer exemplifies the importance of aligning our desires with God's will.

Paul's Prayers for the Churches

The apostle Paul frequently offered supplications for the early churches. This is what he said:

"I have not stopped giving thanks for you, remembering you in my prayers. I keep asking that the God of our Lord Jesus Christ, the glorious Father, may give you the Spirit of wisdom and revelation, so that you may know him better. I pray that the eyes of your heart may be enlightened in order that you may know the hope to which he has called you, the riches of his glorious inheritance in his holy people, and his incomparably great power for us who believe. That power is the same as the mighty strength." **(Ephesians 1:16-19, NIV).**

He prayed for the believers to receive a spirit of wisdom and revelation, that they may know God better. His prayers demonstrate a deep concern for their spiritual growth and well-being.

Conclusion

Supplication and intercession are essential practices in the life of a believer, deepening our relationship with God and fostering a sense of community within the body of Christ. Through supplication, we express our dependence on God, bringing our needs and desires before Him with faith and humility. Intercessory prayer, on the other hand, allows us to stand in the gap for others, seeking God's intervention in their lives and reflecting His love and compassion.

By studying scriptural examples of supplication and intercession, we gain insight into the power and importance of these prayers. As we cultivate a habit of asking and receiving, and commit to praying for others, we grow in our faith and become instruments of God's grace and power in the world. Through persistent and heartfelt prayer, we witness God's transformative work in our lives and the lives of those around us, bringing glory to His name and advancing His kingdom.

Closing Prayer

Gracious and Loving Father,

As we conclude this chapter on "Thanksgiving and Gratitude," our hearts are filled with deep appreciation for the countless blessings You have bestowed upon us. Thank You for the opportunity to reflect on the importance of living a life marked by gratitude. We are in awe of Your goodness, faithfulness, and unending love.

Lord, we thank You for every good gift, for Your provision, protection, and the abundant grace You shower upon us daily. Help us to cultivate a spirit of thanksgiving in all circumstances, recognizing Your hand at work in every aspect of our lives. Teach us to see beyond our challenges and to acknowledge Your presence and blessings, no matter the situation

May our hearts overflow with gratitude, not only for the material blessings but for the spiritual blessings that come from knowing You. Thank You for the gift of salvation, the guidance of the Holy Spirit, and the hope of eternal life through Jesus

Christ. We are grateful for Your steadfast love and for the assurance that You are always with us.

As we move forward, help us to express our gratitude through our words and actions. Let our lives be a testament to Your goodness, inspiring others to see Your light through our thankfulness. Guide us to be mindful of the ways we can bless others, sharing Your love and generosity with those around us.

Thank You, Lord, for the reminder that a grateful heart is a joyful heart. Fill us with the joy that comes from acknowledging Your blessings and responding with praise and thanksgiving. May our gratitude deepen our relationship with You and bring glory to Your name.

In Jesus' name, we pray.

Amen.

Word Puzzles

TYPES AND FORMS OF PRAYER

CROSSWORD

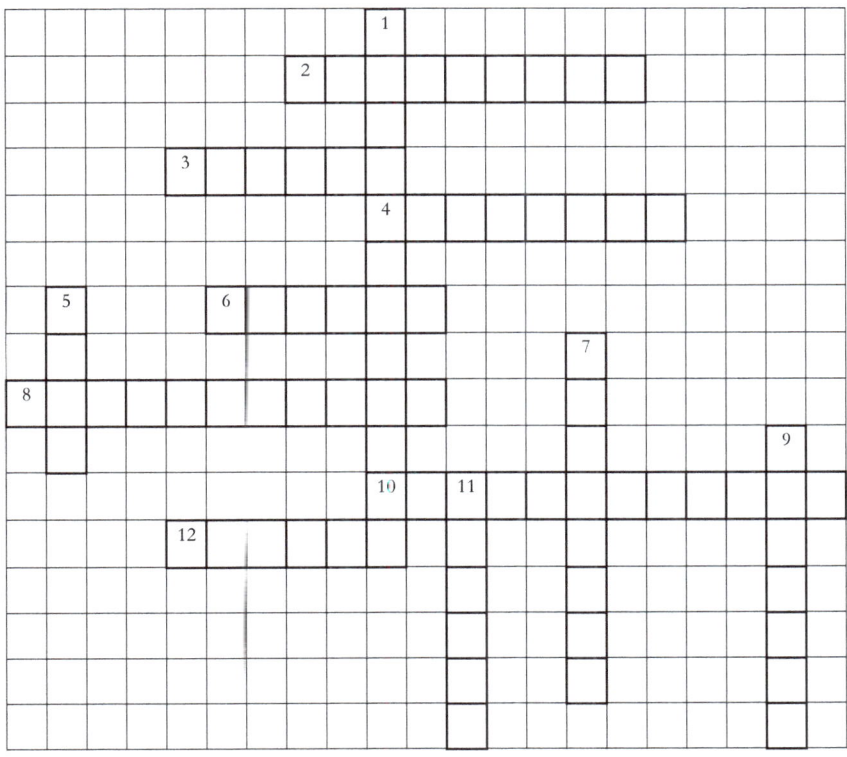

Across

2 THANKFULNESS AND APPRECIATION

3 TO TURN AWAY FROM SIN

4 QUALITY OF BEING HOLY

6 TO HOLD IN HIGH ESTEEM

8 AUTHORITY AND POWER GIVEN TO SOMEONE

10 AN EARNEST PLEA FOR SOMETHING

12 SACRED SONGS IN THE BIBLE

Down

1 LASTING LOYALTY AND TRUSTWORTHINESS

5 A RELIGIOUS SONG

7 THINK DEEPLY ABOUT SOMETHING

9 EXPRESSION OF REVERENCE TO GOD

11 EXPRESSION OF RESPECT AND GRATITUDE

TYPES AND FORMS OF PRAYER
CROSSWORD--ANSWER

Across:
- GRATITUDE
- REPENT
- HOLINESS
- HONOUR
- EMPOWERMENT
- SUPPLICATION
- PSALMS

Down:
- FIGHTFULFILNESS (F-I-T-H-F-U-L-N-E-S-S... FAITHFULNESS)
- HYMN
- MEDITATE
- PRAISE
- WORSHIP

Across

2 THANKFULNESS AND APPRECIATION
3 TO TURN AWAY FROM SIN
4 QUALITY OF BEING HOLY
6 TO HOLD IN HIGH ESTEEM
8 AUTHORITY AND POWER GIVEN TO SOMEONE
10 AN EARNEST PLEA FOR SOMETHING
12 SACRED SONGS IN THE BIBLE

Down

1 LASTING LOYALTY AND TRUSTWORTHINESS
5 A RELIGIOUS SONG
7 THINK DEEPLY ABOUT SOMETHING
9 EXPRESSION OF REVERENCE TO GOD
11 EXPRESSION OF RESPECT AND GRATITUDE

TYPES AND FORMS OF PRAYER WORDSEARCH

```
Q D U I T U E W G S R O L N Q
E G Z P U N O M S K E M W O Z
C R J P Y U E E P B B H O I S
N A A Z X E N M W B O A R T O
A T K P D I S C W N L S S A N
T I A I L U D I O O H H H C G
N T N O U G G U A T P B I I S
E U H M D N R J I R P M P L U
P D Y Z W L M R Q G P A E P K
E E S M E D I T A T I O N P R
R I X B B P P Z A C X J H U J
C J V Q S J U E W F L U M S W
B S S E N L U F H T I A F J X
P E X S E S G I U H Y M N K B
R H Q B Q W U T O U B S U R Z
```

EMPOWMENT	HYMN	SPIRIT
FAITHFULNESS	MEDITATION	SUPPLICATION
GRATITUDE	PRAISE	WORSHIP
HOLINESS	REPENTANCE	
HONOUR	SONGS	

TYPES AND FORMS OF PRAYER
WORDSEARCH--ANSWER

	1	2	3	4	5	6	7	8	9	10	11	12	13	14	15
1	Q	D	U	I	T	U	E	W	G	S	R	O	L	N	Q
2	E	G	Z	P	U	N	O	M	S	K	E	M	W	O	Z
3	C	R	J	P	Y	U	E	E	P	B	B	H	O	I	S
4	N	A	A	Z	X	E	N	M	W	B	O	A	R	T	O
5	A	T	K	P	D	I	S	C	W	N	L	S	S	A	N
6	T	I	A	I	L	U	D	I	O	O	H	H	H	C	G
7	N	T	N	O	U	G	G	U	A	T	P	B	I	I	S
8	E	U	H	M	D	N	R	J	I	R	P	M	P	L	U
9	P	D	Y	Z	W	L	M	R	Q	G	P	A	E	P	K
10	E	E	S	M	E	D	I	T	A	T	I	O	N	P	R
11	R	I	X	B	B	P	P	Z	A	C	X	J	H	U	J
12	C	J	V	Q	S	J	U	E	W	F	L	U	M	S	W
13	B	S	S	E	N	L	U	F	H	T	I	A	F	J	X
14	P	E	X	S	E	S	G	I	U	H	Y	M	N	K	B
15	R	H	Q	B	Q	W	U	T	O	U	B	S	U	R	Z

101

The words below are listed with their starting row and column

EMPOWMENT 9:13

HYMN 14:10

SPIRIT 12:5

FAITHFULNESS 13:13

MEDITATION 10:4

SUPPLICATION 12:14

GRATITUDE 2:2

PRAISE 9:11

WORSHIP 2:13

HOLINESS 8:3

REPENTANCE 11:1

HONOUR 3:12

SONGS 3:15

PART III
THE PRACTICE OF PRAYER

CHAPTER 10

DEVELOPING A PRAYER ROUTINE

Keeping a prayer journal can deepen your relationship with God

Opening Prayer

Heavenly Father,

As we begin this chapter on "Developing a Prayer Life," we come before You with open hearts and a deep desire to draw closer to You through prayer. Thank You for the gift of prayer, through which we can communicate with You, seek Your guidance, and experience Your presence. We are grateful for the opportunity to grow in our relationship with You.

Lord, we ask for Your wisdom and direction as we explore how to cultivate a meaningful and consistent prayer life. Open our minds to understand the importance of prayer and the ways it can transform our lives. Help us to establish habits that nurture our spiritual growth and deepen our connection with You.

May Your Holy Spirit be our guide and teacher as we embark on this journey. Illuminate the principles and practices that will help us develop a rich and fulfilling prayer life. Encourage us to be intentional in setting aside time for prayer, and grant us the discipline to persevere even when it feels challenging.

Remove any distractions, doubts, or fears that may hinder our commitment to prayer. Fill us with a longing to spend time in Your presence, to listen to Your voice, and to pour out our hearts before You. Let our prayer life be marked by authenticity, sincerity, and a deep sense of communion with You.

Lord, as we study and reflect on the importance of developing a prayer life, may we be inspired and equipped to make prayer a central part of our daily routine. Let our prayers be a source of strength, comfort, and guidance, drawing us ever closer to You and aligning our hearts with Your will.

Thank You for Your patience and grace as we grow in this area. May this chapter be a stepping stone to a deeper, more vibrant prayer life that brings glory to Your name.

In the precious name of Jesus Christ, our Lord and Saviour, we pray.

Amen.

Introduction

Prayer should always be taken seriously. Developing a prayer routine is crucial for nurturing a deep and consistent relationship with God. A structured prayer life helps to anchor our faith, providing a rhythm that keeps us connected to God amidst the busyness of daily life. By establishing regular prayer practices, we cultivate a habit of seeking God's presence, guidance, and support. This chapter will explore practical steps to develop a meaningful prayer routine, ensuring that our spiritual lives remain vibrant and grounded. We will examine the following themes: establishing regular prayer times, creating a prayer journal, and overcoming distractions.

Establishing Regular Prayer Times

Establishing regular prayer times is the foundation of a consistent prayer routine. Setting aside specific times each day for prayer helps to prioritize our relationship with God and ensures that prayer becomes an integral part of our daily lives.

Choose a Time that Works for You

Remember that God is always available. He is never too busy to listen to our prayers. Select a time of day when you can be consistent and focused. For some, early morning provides a quiet and undisturbed period to connect with God before the day begins. For others, the evening may be more suitable, allowing for reflection and winding down after the day's activities.

Start Small and Be Realistic

Begin with manageable goals to avoid feeling overwhelmed. Even setting aside 10-15 minutes for focused prayer can make a significant difference. As the habit becomes established, you can gradually increase the time.

Create a Sacred Space

Designate a specific place for prayer that is free from distractions. This could be a quiet corner in your home, a spot in nature, or any place where you feel comfortable and can focus on God.

Incorporate Prayer into Daily Activities

Integrate prayer into your daily routines. For instance, you can pray during your commute, while doing household chores, or during breaks at work. These moments can become opportunities to connect with God and maintain a prayerful attitude throughout the day. Whatever the circumstances under which you pray, always remember to be reverent.

Set Reminders

Use alarms or reminders on your phone or calendar to prompt you to pray. This helps to build the habit and ensures that prayer becomes a regular part of your schedule.

Creating a Prayer Journal

A prayer journal is a valuable tool for organizing your thoughts, recording your prayers, and tracking God's answers. It helps to deepen your prayer life by providing a tangible way to reflect on your spiritual journey.

Choose a Journal

Select a journal that you find appealing and comfortable to write in. It could be a simple notebook, a dedicated prayer journal, or a digital app.

Organize Your Entries

Structure your journal in a way that works for you. You might want to divide it into sections, such as prayers of adoration, confession, thanksgiving, and supplication. Alternatively, you can use it as a daily log, recording your prayers and reflections for each day.

Record Specific Prayers

Write down your prayers in detail. Be specific about what you are asking for, expressing your thoughts and feelings to God. This practice helps to clarify your prayers and makes it easier to see how God answers them over time.

Reflect and Review

Review your journal entries regularly to reflect on your spiritual growth and recognize answered prayers. This reflection fosters gratitude and strengthens your faith as you see how God has been working in your life.

Include Scripture

Incorporate Bible verses into your journal that relate to your prayers. This helps to ground your prayers in God's word and provides additional inspiration and guidance.

Overcoming Distractions

Distractions are a common challenge in maintaining a consistent prayer routine. Overcoming these distractions requires intentional strategies to keep your focus on God.

Identify Common Distractions

Recognize the things that most often draw your attention away during prayer. These could be external factors, such as noise or interruptions, or internal factors, such as wandering thoughts or worries.

Create a Distraction-Free Environment:

Choose a quiet and comfortable place for prayer. Inform those around you of your prayer time to minimize interruptions. If necessary, use noise-canceling headphones or calming background music to help you focus.

Practice Mindfulness

When distractions arise, gently bring your focus back to God. Techniques such as deep breathing, repeating a centering word or phrase, or focusing on a specific attribute of God can help to refocus your mind.

Use Written Prayers or Prayer Guides

Having a written prayer or guide can help keep you focused. Prayer books, devotionals, or guided meditation apps can provide structure and help you stay on track.

Conclusion

Developing a prayer routine is a journey that requires intentionality, commitment, and flexibility. By establishing regular prayer times, creating a prayer journal, and overcoming distractions, we can cultivate a deep and consistent prayer life. This routine not only strengthens our relationship with God but also enhances our spiritual growth and resilience. As we persevere in prayer, we open ourselves to the transforming power of God's presence, experiencing His guidance, comfort, and peace in every aspect of our lives.

Closing Prayer

Heavenly Father,

As we conclude this chapter on "Developing a Prayer Routine," we come before You with grateful hearts, thankful for the wisdom and guidance You have provided. We recognize the importance of establishing a consistent and meaningful prayer life, and we ask for Your help in making this a reality in our daily lives.

Lord, we desire to draw closer to You through regular and heartfelt prayer. Teach us to prioritize our time with You, to set aside moments each day to commune with You, and to make prayer an integral part of our routine. Help us to be disciplined and committed, even when life gets busy and distractions abound.

Fill us with the Holy Spirit, who intercedes for us and guides our prayers. Give us the words to say when we do not know how to pray and help us to listen for Your voice in the stillness. May our prayer routine be a source of strength, comfort, and guidance as we seek to live according to Your will.

We ask for Your grace to persevere in prayer, even when we face challenges and discouragement. Remind us that our prayers are heard and that You are always near, ready to respond with love and wisdom. Strengthen our faith, so that we may trust in Your perfect timing and Your good plans for our lives.

Lord, may our prayer routine not be a mere habit, but a vibrant and dynamic relationship with You. Let it be a time of growth, transformation, and deepening intimacy with You. As we commit to regular prayer, may we experience the fullness of Your presence and the joy of walking closely with You.

Thank You, Father, for the gift of prayer and for the opportunity to develop a deeper connection with You. We dedicate our efforts to establishing a prayer routine to Your glory, trusting that You will guide us every step of the way.

In the name of Jesus Christ, our Saviour and Lord, we pray.

Amen.

CHAPTER 11
PRAYING WITH SCRIPTURE

Use Biblical verses in your communication with the Father.

Opening Prayer

Heavenly Father,

As we begin this chapter on "Praying with Scripture," we come before You with hearts full of anticipation and reverence for Your Holy Word. Thank You for the Bible, Your living and active Word that guides, instructs, and nourishes our souls. We are grateful for the opportunity to learn how to incorporate Scripture into our prayer lives, deepening our connection with You.

Lord, we ask for Your wisdom and insight as we explore the power and beauty of praying with Scripture. Open our hearts and minds to understand how Your Word can shape and enhance our prayers. Teach us to approach the Bible with humility and expectation, ready to hear Your voice and be transformed by Your truth.

May Your Holy Spirit be our guide and teacher as we delve into this practice. Illuminate the scriptures we will study and show us how to pray them with faith and sincerity. Help us to internalize Your Word, allowing it to dwell richly in our hearts and inform our prayers. May Your Word become a wellspring of inspiration, comfort, and strength in our times of prayer.

Remove any barriers or distractions that may prevent us from fully engaging with Your Word in prayer. Grant us the discipline to meditate on Scripture and the discernment to apply its truths to our lives. Let our prayers be infused with the power and authority of Your Word, aligning our hearts with Your will and purposes.

Lord, as we journey through this chapter, may we be inspired and equipped to make praying with Scripture a regular and meaningful part of our spiritual practice. Let Your Word be a lamp to our feet and a light to our path, guiding us in our prayers and drawing us closer to You.

Thank You for the gift of Your Word and for the privilege of communing with You through prayer. May this chapter deepen our love for Scripture and enrich our prayer lives in profound ways.

In the precious name of Jesus Christ, our Lord and Savior, we pray.

Amen.

Introduction

Praying with Scripture is a powerful practice that bridges the gap between the divine Word and our personal conversation with God. It transforms our prayer life, grounding it in the infallible truths of the Bible and ensuring our requests, praises, and confessions align with God's will. This chapter explores how to incorporate Scripture into prayer, deepening our spiritual connection and enriching our faith journey. We explore the following topics: using the psalms in prayer, praying the promises of God, and scripture-based prayer techniques.

Using the Psalms in Prayer

The Book of Psalms is often called the prayer book of the Bible. Written by various authors, including King David, the Psalms express a wide range of human emotions, from joy and gratitude to sorrow and repentance. Using the Psalms in prayer can be particularly comforting because they give voice to our feelings and help us articulate our innermost thoughts to God.

How to Use the Psalms in Prayer

Identify Your Current Emotion: Choose a psalm that resonates with your current emotional state. If you are joyful, Psalm 100 is an excellent choice. For times of sorrow, Psalm 42 provides solace.

Personalize the Psalm: As you read the Psalm, personalize it by inserting your name or the names of others for whom you are praying. For example, in Psalm 23, "The Lord is my shepherd," you might say, "The Lord is John's shepherd."

Pray the Psalm Verbally: Speak the Psalm aloud as a prayer. This practice can help you internalize the words and make them a part of your own prayer language.

Meditate on Key Verses: Reflect on verses that particularly speak to you. Ask God to reveal deeper insights and how they apply to your life.

Praying the Promises of God

God's promises are scattered throughout Scripture, providing hope, encouragement, and assurance. Praying these promises can strengthen our faith, remind us of God's faithfulness, and align our desires with His plans.

Steps to Pray God's Promises

Identify Relevant Promises: Search the Bible for promises that pertain to your situation. For instance, if you are feeling anxious, Philippians 4:6-7 offers peace: "Do not be anxious about anything..."

Claim the Promises in Prayer: Acknowledge these promises in your prayer. For example, "Lord, You have promised that You will never leave me nor forsake me (Hebrews 13:5). I trust in Your presence and Your guidance."

Express Gratitude: Thank God for His promises and express your trust in His faithfulness to fulfil them.

Live in Expectation: Let the promises of God transform your mindset. Live in the expectation that God will honour His Word.

Scripture-Based Prayer Technique

Developing a Scripture-based prayer technique involves more than merely reciting verses. It requires intentionality, reflection, and a heart aligned with God's will.

Steps for Scripture-Based Prayer

Choose a Passage: Select a passage that speaks to your current need or situation.

Read and Reflect: Read the passage several times, reflecting on its meaning and how it applies to your life. Consider the context and the original audience.

Write Your Prayer: Based on the passage, write out a prayer. Incorporate the specific language and themes of the Scripture. For example, using Ephesians 3:14-21, you might pray for strength, love, and the fullness of God's presence.

Pray Aloud: Speak your written prayer aloud, allowing the words to resonate in your heart and mind.

Listen and Respond: After praying, take a moment to listen for God's response. Reflect on any thoughts or impressions that come to mind and respond in prayer.

Conclusion

Praying with Scripture transforms our communication with God, rooting it in His unchanging Word and bringing us into closer alignment with His will. Whether using the Psalms to express our emotions, claiming God's promises, or developing a Scripture-based prayer technique, the practice enriches our spiritual lives and deepens our relationship with the Creator. As we incorporate Scripture into our prayers, we experience the power of God's Word in a personal and transformative way, guiding us on our faith journey.

Closing Prayer

Heavenly Father,

As we conclude this chapter on "Praying with Scripture," we are filled with gratitude for the ways You have revealed Yourself through Your Word. Thank You for the rich and living scriptures that guide us, comfort us, and draw us closer to You. We are grateful for the opportunity to deepen our prayer life through the sacred words of the Bible.

Lord, help us to integrate the practice of praying with Scripture into our daily lives. Open our hearts and minds to the truths found in Your Word, and teach us to meditate on these truths as we come before You in prayer. May the scriptures inspire our prayers, providing us with words when we have none and illuminating Your will for our lives.

Grant us wisdom and understanding as we read and pray through the Bible. Let Your Word be a lamp to our feet and a light to our path, guiding us in every decision and circumstance. May our prayers be enriched by the promises, praises, and teachings found in the scriptures, aligning our hearts with Yours.

We ask for the Holy Spirit's guidance as we engage with Your Word in prayer. Help us to discern Your voice and to respond in obedience to Your call. May the scriptures shape our prayers, transforming our hearts and minds to reflect Your love, grace, and truth.

Lord, we are grateful for the living and active Word of God that speaks into every aspect of our lives. As we continue to pray with Scripture, may we grow in our relationship with You, finding strength, comfort, and direction in Your holy words.

Thank You for the gift of Your Word and for the privilege of communing with You through prayer. May our lives be a testament to the power of praying with Scripture, bringing glory to Your name.

In the name of Jesus Christ, our Lord and Saviour, we pray.

Amen.

CHAPTER 12

PRAYER ON THE SABBATH DAY

A day of rest and gladness

Opening Prayer

Heavenly Father,

As we begin this exploration of prayer on the Sabbath, we invite Your presence to guide our thoughts and open our hearts. Thank You for the gift of the Sabbath, a day set apart for rest and communion with You. Help us to understand the depth and beauty of this sacred time, and teach us how to honour it through prayer. May our study deepen our relationship with You, refresh our spirits, and inspire us to embrace the Sabbath with renewed devotion. Fill us with Your peace, wisdom, and grace as we seek to draw closer to You on this holy day. In Jesus' name, we pray.

Amen.

Introduction

The Sabbath, a day set aside for rest and spiritual rejuvenation, holds profound significance in the Judeo-Christian tradition. Rooted in the creation narrative where God rested on the seventh day, the Sabbath is a time for believers to pause, reflect, and renew their connection with the Divine. One of the most enriching ways to honour this sacred time is through prayer. Prayer on the Sabbath is not merely a ritualistic practice but an invitation to experience deeper communion with God, to seek His presence, and to find rest for our souls. In this chapter, we will explore the biblical foundations of the Sabbath, the role of prayer in observing this holy day, and practical ways to incorporate meaningful prayer into your Sabbath observance.

Biblical Foundations of the Sabbath

The Creation Account

The concept of the Sabbath is first introduced in Genesis 2:2-3, where God rests on the seventh day after the work of creation. This act of divine rest establishes a pattern for humanity, signaling the importance of setting aside time to cease from labour and delight in God's creation.

The Fourth Commandment

The Sabbath is enshrined in the Ten Commandments, specifically in Exodus 20:8-11. Here, God commands His people to remember the Sabbath day and keep it holy. This commandment emphasizes rest, not only for individuals but also for their households, servants, and even animals, highlighting the universal need for rest and restoration.

Remember the Sabbath day by keeping it holy. Six days you shall labor and do all your work, but the seventh day is a sabbath to the LORD your God. On it you shall not do any work, neither you, nor your son or daughter, nor your male or female servant, nor your animals, nor any foreigner residing in your towns. For in six days the LORD made the heavens and the earth, the sea, and all that is in them, but he rested on the seventh day. Therefore the LORD blessed the Sabbath day and made it holy.

Jesus and the Sabbath

In the New Testament, Jesus redefines and enriches the understanding of the Sabbath. He emphasizes that the Sabbath was made for man, not man for the Sabbath (Mark 2:27), and demonstrates through His actions that it is a day for doing good, healing, and restoring (Mark 3:1-6). Jesus' approach underscores the Sabbath's role as a time for holistic well-being, including physical rest and spiritual renewal through prayer.

The Role of Prayer on the Sabbath

A Day for Reflection

The Sabbath provides a unique opportunity for believers to reflect on God's goodness, creation, and their own lives. Prayer is a vital tool for this reflection. Through prayer, believers can express gratitude for the blessings received during the week, seek forgiveness for their shortcomings, and ask for guidance for the days ahead.

Communing with God

Prayer on the Sabbath allows believers to deepen their relationship with God. It is a time to set aside the distractions of daily life and focus solely on the Divine. This communion can take many forms, including silent meditation, spoken prayers, and reading or reciting Scripture.

Restorative Prayer

The Sabbath is a day of rest, and prayer plays a crucial role in spiritual restoration. Engaging in prayers that focus on God's peace, presence, and promises can bring about a sense of inner calm and renewal. This spiritual rest is essential for maintaining a healthy and balanced life.

Practical Ways to Incorporate Prayer on the Sabbath

Morning Prayer

Begin the Sabbath morning with a dedicated time of prayer. This could include reading a psalm, offering thanks for the gift of rest, and asking God to guide your reflections and activities throughout the day. Morning prayer sets a spiritual tone for the rest of the day.

Family Prayer

If you observe the Sabbath with your family, consider incorporating family prayer into your day. This could involve reading Scripture together, sharing prayer requests, and thanking God for His blessings as a family unit. Family prayer fosters unity and shared spiritual growth.

Nature Prayer Walks

Take advantage of the restful nature of the Sabbath by going on a prayer walk in a natural setting. Use this time to marvel at God's creation, pray for the environment, and find inspiration in the beauty around you. Nature walks can enhance your sense of connection to God and His creation.

Reflective Journaling

Journaling can be a powerful form of prayer on the Sabbath. Spend time writing down your thoughts, prayers, and reflections. Consider what God has taught you during the week and what you hope to focus on in the coming days. Journaling helps to clarify your spiritual journey and provides a record of God's faithfulness.

Evening Prayer

Conclude the Sabbath with an evening prayer. Reflect on the day, give thanks for the rest and renewal you've experienced, and pray for the week ahead. Evening prayer serves as a bookend to your Sabbath observance, reinforcing the spiritual benefits of the day.

Conclusion

Prayer on the Sabbath is a transformative practice that allows believers to enter into a deeper relationship with God. Rooted in biblical tradition and enriched by the teachings of Jesus, the Sabbath offers a dedicated time for rest, reflection, and renewal through prayer. By incorporating various forms of prayer into your Sabbath observance—whether through morning devotions, family prayer, nature walks, journaling, or evening reflections—you can experience the full spiritual richness of this holy day. As we embrace the Sabbath with intentionality and reverence, may we find our souls refreshed, our spirits renewed, and our connection to the Divine strengthened.

Closing Prayer

Gracious and Loving Father,

As we conclude this chapter on Prayer on the Sabbath, we thank You for the insights and wisdom You have imparted to us. We are grateful for the Sabbath, a divine gift of rest and renewal, and for the opportunity to deepen our understanding of how to honour this holy day through prayer. Help us to carry forward the lessons we have learned, incorporating them into our Sabbath observance with intentionality and reverence. May our prayers on the Sabbath draw us closer to You, filling us with Your peace, love, and presence.

Lord, we ask that You continue to guide us in our spiritual journey, not just on the Sabbath, but every day of our lives. Teach us to find rest in You, to seek Your face in moments of quiet reflection, and to embrace the rhythm of rest You have designed for our well-being. As we go forth, may the practice of Sabbath prayer transform our hearts, renew our spirits, and strengthen our faith. We entrust our lives into

Your loving hands, knowing that You are our ultimate source of rest and restoration. In Jesus' precious name, we pray.

Amen.

CHAPTER 13

PRAYING IN TONGUES

People spoke in tongues on the Day of Pentecost.

Opening Prayer

Heavenly Father,

We come before You with humble hearts, seeking to understand and embrace the gifts You have bestowed upon us through Your Holy Spirit. As we delve into the mystery and power of praying in tongues, we ask for Your wisdom and guidance. Open our minds to comprehend Your Word and open our spirits to receive Your truth. May this exploration deepen our relationship with You and enrich our prayer lives. Fill us with Your presence, Lord, and lead us into a deeper experience of Your love and grace. In Jesus' name, we pray.

Amen.

Introduction

Praying in tongues, also known as glossolalia, is a practice that has sparked much curiosity, debate, and devotion within the Christian community. This spiritual gift, described in the New Testament, particularly in the books of Acts and 1 Corinthians, involves speaking in an unknown language as a form of prayer and worship. For some, it is a deeply personal and mystical experience, providing a direct connection to God beyond the limitations of human language. For others, it raises questions about its purpose, authenticity, and place in modern Christian practice. In this chapter, we will explore the biblical foundations of praying in tongues, its theological significance, and practical implications for contemporary believers.

Biblical Foundations

Old Testament Foreshadowing

Although praying in tongues is primarily a New Testament phenomenon, there are hints and foreshadowings in the Old Testament. For instance, the Tower of Babel (Genesis 11:1-9) demonstrates the diversity of languages and the power of speech, while the prophetic writings (e.g., Isaiah 28:11) hint at a future time when God would speak to His people through "stammering lips and another tongue."

The Day of Pentecost

The most notable occurrence of praying in tongues is recorded in Acts 2:1-4, during the Day of Pentecost. The Holy Spirit descended upon the apostles, enabling them to speak in various languages. This event marked the birth of the Christian church and symbolized the universal nature of the gospel, transcending cultural and linguistic barriers.

Paul's Teachings in 1 Corinthians

The Apostle Paul provides extensive teaching on praying in tongues in 1 Corinthians 12-14. He identifies it as one of the spiritual gifts bestowed by the Holy Spirit (1 Corinthians 12:10). Paul emphasizes that while tongues can edify the individual believer (1 Corinthians 14:4), it should be practiced in an orderly manner within the church to avoid confusion (1 Corinthians 14:27-28). He also highlights the importance of interpretation so that the church community can be edified (1 Corinthians 14:13).

Theological Significance

A Sign of the Holy Spirit

Praying in tongues is considered a sign of the Holy Spirit's presence and activity. It serves as a manifestation of the Spirit's power and a confirmation of God's work within a believer's life. This gift is often associated with the baptism of the Holy Spirit, a deeper spiritual experience beyond initial conversion.

Personal Edification

One of the primary purposes of praying in tongues is personal edification. Paul notes that speaking in tongues builds up the individual (1 Corinthians 14:4). This practice allows believers to bypass their cognitive limitations and connect with God on a spiritual level, expressing prayers and praises that words cannot fully convey.

Intercession and Spiritual Warfare

Praying in tongues is also seen as a powerful tool for intercession and spiritual warfare. According to Romans 8:26-27, the Holy Spirit intercedes for believers with groanings too deep for words. Praying in tongues can be a way for the Spirit to intercede through us, aligning our prayers with God's perfect will. It is believed to strengthen believers in spiritual battles, providing a divine means of combating evil forces.

Practical Implications

Developing the Gift

For those seeking to develop the gift of praying in tongues, it is important to cultivate a heart of openness and receptivity to the Holy Spirit. Engaging in regular prayer, worship, and immersion in Scripture can create an environment conducive to receiving and exercising this gift. It is also beneficial to seek guidance from mature believers who have experience with this practice.

Using the Gift in Corporate Worship

When praying in tongues within a corporate worship setting, it is essential to follow Paul's instructions for order and clarity. If tongues are spoken publicly, there should be an interpretation to ensure that the entire congregation can be edified (1 Corinthians 14:27-28). Leaders should create a respectful and supportive atmosphere where spiritual gifts can be exercised appropriately.

Addressing Concerns and Misconceptions

Praying in tongues can sometimes be misunderstood or misused, leading to confusion or division within the church. It is crucial to address concerns and misconceptions with sensitivity and biblical insight. Teaching on the nature, purpose, and proper use of spiritual gifts can help demystify the practice and promote unity.

Conclusion

Praying in tongues remains a profound and multifaceted aspect of Christian spirituality. Rooted in biblical teachings and enriched by centuries of church tradition, it offers believers a unique way to connect with God, edify themselves, and engage in spiritual intercession. While it may not be universally practiced or understood, it holds significant value for those who embrace it as a gift from the Holy Spirit. As we continue to seek a deeper relationship with God, may we remain open to the diverse ways He chooses to work within and through us, including the mysterious and powerful practice of praying in tongues.

Closing Prayer

Gracious God,

We thank You for the insights and understanding You have granted us as we have studied the gift of praying in tongues. May the truths we have discovered take root in our hearts and bear fruit in our lives. Help us to approach this gift with reverence, openness, and a desire to draw closer to You. Strengthen our faith and fill us with Your Holy Spirit, so that our prayers may rise to You in power and purity. As we continue our journey with You, may we always seek to glorify Your name in all that we do. In Jesus' name, we pray.

Amen.

CHAPTER 14

PRAYER IN THE WORKPLACE

Prayer in the workplace provides spiritual strength.

Opening Prayer

As we embark on this exploration of prayer in the workplace, we invite Your presence to guide our thoughts and hearts. We thank You for the gift of work and the opportunities it provides to serve You and others. Open our minds to understand how we can integrate prayer into our daily professional lives, seeking Your wisdom, strength, and peace in every task we undertake. May this chapter inspire us to bring our faith into the workplace, transforming it into a place of joy, collaboration, and purpose. Bless our efforts to honor You in all that we do, and may Your presence be felt in our work environment. In Jesus' name, we pray.

Amen.

Introduction

In today's fast-paced and often stressful work environments, finding moments of peace and spiritual connection can be challenging. However, prayer in the workplace offers a powerful way to integrate faith into daily professional life, providing guidance, strength, and a sense of purpose. This chapter explores the significance, challenges, and practical ways of incorporating prayer into the workplace. Through biblical insights and practical tips, we aim to show how prayer can transform not only individual experiences but also the entire workplace culture, fostering a sense of community and shared values.

The Significance of Prayer in the Workplace

Acknowledging God's Presence

Prayer in the workplace begins with the recognition that God is present in all aspects of our lives, including our professional endeavours. This acknowledgment can transform how we perceive our work, seeing it not merely as a means to earn a living but as a vocation where we can glorify God. As the Apostle Paul reminds us:

"Whatever you do, work heartily, as for the Lord and not for men, knowing that from the Lord you will receive the inheritance as your reward. You are serving the Lord Christ." **(Colossians 3:23-24).**

Seeking Guidance and Wisdom

The workplace often presents complex challenges and decisions. Prayer is a way to seek God's guidance and wisdom in navigating these situations. James encourages believers:

"If any of you lacks wisdom, let him ask God, who gives generously to all without reproach, and it will be given him." **(James 1:5).**

Through prayer, employees and employers alike can find divine insight and clarity, leading to more thoughtful and ethical decision-making.

Building Community and Unity

Prayer has the power to bring people together, fostering a sense of community and unity in the workplace. When colleagues pray together, it creates bonds of mutual respect and support. This communal aspect of prayer can help break down barriers, resolve conflicts, and promote a collaborative and positive work environment. In Matthew 18:20, Jesus assures, "For where two or three are gathered in my name, there am I among them."

Practical Ways to Incorporate Prayer in the Workplace

Personal Prayer

One of the simplest ways to incorporate prayer into the workplace is through personal prayer. This can be done at various times throughout the day:

Morning Prayer: Start your day with a brief prayer, asking for God's presence, guidance, and blessing on your work.

Moments of Silence: Take short breaks to pray silently, especially during stressful or challenging times.

End-of-Day Reflection: Conclude your workday with a prayer of gratitude for the accomplishments and lessons learned, seeking peace and rest for the evening.

Prayer Groups and Meetings

Forming prayer groups or scheduling regular prayer meetings can create a supportive spiritual community within the workplace. Here are some steps to initiate this:

Gather Interest: Identify colleagues who are interested in participating in a prayer group.

Set a Schedule: Choose a consistent time and place for meetings, such as before work, during lunch breaks, or after work.

Create a Structure: Have a flexible structure for the meetings, including sharing prayer requests, reading Scripture, and praying together.

Prayer Spaces

If possible, create or designate a quiet space for prayer and reflection within the workplace. This space should be accessible and respectful of all employees' need for privacy and quiet. A dedicated prayer room can provide a sanctuary for employees to retreat, pray, and recharge during their workday.

Integrating Prayer into Meetings

Incorporating prayer into regular business meetings can be a way to acknowledge God's presence and seek His guidance in corporate decisions. This could be a brief opening or closing prayer, asking for wisdom, clarity, and unity among the team. Ensure that this practice is inclusive and respectful of all participants' beliefs.

Addressing Challenges and Considerations

Respecting Diversity

In a diverse workplace, it is essential to respect and accommodate different religious beliefs and practices. Prayer in the workplace should be inclusive and considerate of all employees. Encourage voluntary participation and ensure that no one feels pressured or excluded.

Navigating Legal and Ethical Boundaries

Be mindful of legal and ethical considerations when incorporating prayer into the workplace. Familiarize yourself with company policies and relevant labour laws regarding religious expression. It is crucial to maintain a balance that respects both individual freedoms and professional boundaries.

Overcoming Resistance

Introducing prayer into the workplace may face resistance from some employees or management. Address concerns with sensitivity and openness, emphasizing the voluntary nature of participation and the potential benefits for personal and collective well-being. Sharing positive testimonies and success stories can help build acceptance and enthusiasm.

Conclusion

Prayer in the workplace is a profound way to integrate faith into our professional lives, providing spiritual support, guidance, and a sense of purpose. By acknowledging God's presence, seeking His wisdom, and building community through prayer, we can transform our work environment into a space of collaboration, respect, and mutual support. Despite the challenges, the benefits of incorporating prayer into the workplace are far-reaching, fostering personal growth, ethical decision-making, and a positive, unified workplace culture. As we strive to live out our faith in every aspect of our lives, may we find in prayer a powerful tool to navigate the complexities of the workplace, bringing glory to God in all that we do.

Closing Prayer

Gracious Father,

As we conclude this chapter on prayer in the workplace, we thank You for the insights and wisdom You have imparted to us. We are grateful for the reminder that Your presence is with us in every aspect of our lives, including our professional endeavours. Help us to carry forward the lessons we have learned, integrating prayer into our workdays with intentionality and faith. May our efforts to seek You in our workplaces bring about a spirit of unity, peace, and purpose among our colleagues. Strengthen us to be beacons of Your love and grace in all that we do, and may our work bring glory to Your name. In Jesus' name, we pray.

Amen.

CHAPTER 15

CORPORATE PRAYER

Corporate prayer unites God's people.

Opening Prayer

Gracious and Almighty God,

As we begin this chapter on "Corporate Prayer," we come before You with hearts filled with gratitude for the gift of communal prayer. Thank You for the opportunity to gather with fellow believers, united in spirit and purpose, to seek Your face and lift our voices together in prayer. We are grateful for the strength, encouragement, and sense of community that corporate prayer brings.

Lord, we ask for Your presence and guidance as we explore the significance and power of praying together as the body of Christ. Open our hearts to understand the unique blessings and responsibilities that come with corporate prayer. Help us to see the ways in which You move mightily when Your people come together in unity and faith.

Grant that Your Holy Spirit be our teacher and guide as we delve into this practice. Illuminate the scriptures and principles that highlight the importance of corporate prayer. Show us how to pray together effectively, with humility, sincerity, and a shared desire to glorify Your name. Help us to listen to one another, support each other, and grow in our collective faith.

Remove any barriers or divisions that may hinder our unity in prayer. Fill us with a spirit of love, compassion, and cooperation as we join our hearts and voices in prayer. May our corporate prayers be a powerful witness to the world of Your love and the strength of our fellowship.

Lord, as we journey through this chapter, may we be inspired and equipped to participate fully in the practice of corporate prayer. Let our times of communal prayer be marked by Your presence and power, drawing us closer to You and to one another. May our prayers bring about transformation in our lives, our churches, and our communities.

Thank You for the privilege of praying together as Your people. May this chapter deepen our understanding and commitment to corporate prayer, and may it enrich our spiritual lives in profound ways.

In the precious name of Jesus Christ, our Lord and Savior, we pray.

Amen.

Introduction

Corporate prayer, or praying together as a community, has been a foundational practice in the Christian faith since the early church. It is a powerful expression of unity, shared faith, and collective intercession. Corporate prayer brings believers together, fostering a sense of communal strength and support as they seek God's guidance, provision, and intervention. This chapter delves into the significance of corporate prayer, its benefits, and practical ways to organize and participate in group prayer within the church.

The Power of Praying Together

Praying together amplifies the voices of believers, creating a harmonious chorus that reaches the throne of God. The Bible emphasizes the importance and power of collective prayer, promising that when believers come together in agreement, their prayers carry extraordinary power.

Biblical Foundations

Matthew 18:19-20

"Again, truly I tell you that if two of you on earth agree about anything they ask for, it will be done for them by my Father in heaven. For where two or three gather in my name, there am I with them."

This passage underscores the assurance of God's presence and the effectiveness of unified prayer.

Acts 2:42

"They devoted themselves to the apostles' teaching and to fellowship, to the breaking of bread and to prayer."

The early church prioritized communal prayer, reflecting its integral role in their spiritual lives.

Benefits of Corporate Prayer

Unity and Fellowship: Corporate prayer fosters unity among believers, breaking down barriers and building stronger relationships within the body of Christ.

Encouragement and Support: Praying together provides encouragement, as individuals share their burdens and witness the faith and testimonies of others.

Spiritual Growth: It promotes spiritual growth, as participants learn from each other's prayers, deepen their understanding of God's Word, and experience the Holy Spirit's work collectively.

Organizing Prayer Groups

Prayer groups are an effective way to facilitate corporate prayer within a church community. These smaller gatherings can focus on specific needs, interests, or demographics, providing a more intimate setting for prayer and fellowship.

Steps to Organize a Prayer Group

Identify the Purpose: Determine the focus of the prayer group. It could be a general prayer group, or it might focus on specific areas like intercessory prayer, prayer for families, or prayer for missions.

Recruit Leaders: Select leaders who are passionate about prayer and capable of guiding and nurturing the group. These leaders should be spiritually mature and committed to the group's purpose.

Set a Schedule: Choose a regular meeting time and place that is convenient for participants. Consistency is key to building a committed group.

Promote the Group: Use church announcements, bulletins, and social media to inform the congregation about the prayer group. Encourage members to invite others.

Structure the Meetings: Plan a structure for the meetings, including time for worship, sharing prayer requests, and dedicated prayer time. Flexibility is important, allowing the Holy Spirit to lead.

Church-Wide Prayer Initiatives

Beyond smaller prayer groups, church-wide prayer initiatives can mobilize the entire congregation to pray together. These initiatives can take various forms, from special prayer events to ongoing campaigns that engage the whole church.

Types of Church-Wide Prayer Initiatives

Prayer Vigils: Organize all-night or extended prayer vigils where members sign up for time slots to ensure continuous prayer. These can focus on specific needs, crises, or spiritual renewal.

Prayer Chains: Create a prayer chain where individuals commit to praying for a specific need at designated times. This ensures continuous prayer coverage and collective intercession.

Monthly Prayer Focus: Designate a specific prayer focus each month, encouraging the congregation to pray for a particular topic, such as missions, community outreach, or church leadership.

Prayer Walks: Arrange prayer walks around the church, neighbourhood, or city, interceding for the community, local authorities, and pressing social issues.

Fasting and Prayer: Call for a time of fasting and prayer, encouraging members to set aside specific days to fast and seek God earnestly.

Implementing Church-Wide Initiatives

Leadership Support: Ensure the church leadership is fully supportive and involved in promoting and participating in the initiatives.

Communication: Clearly communicate the purpose, schedule, and expectations to the congregation. Use various channels to reach as many people as possible.

Resources: Provide resources such as prayer guides, suggested Scriptures, and specific prayer points to help members participate effectively.

Feedback and Testimonies: Encourage members to share testimonies and feedback on how the prayer initiatives have impacted their lives and the church. This can inspire and motivate others to participate.

Conclusion

Corporate prayer is a vital aspect of the Christian faith, bringing believers together to seek God's face, intercede for one another, and experience His power collectively. Whether through prayer groups or church-wide initiatives, the practice of praying together strengthens the church, fosters unity, and deepens the spiritual lives of its members. As we commit to corporate prayer, we open ourselves to the transformative work of the Holy Spirit, witnessing the miraculous and experiencing the fullness of God's presence in our midst.

Closing Prayer

Almighty and Loving Father,

As we conclude this chapter on "Corporate Prayer," we give You thanks for the profound truths and insights we have gained about praying together as a community of believers. We are grateful for the gift of corporate prayer, which unites us in faith, strengthens our fellowship, and draws us closer to You as one body.

Lord, we ask that You help us to embrace the power and importance of praying together. Fill our hearts with a genuine love for one another and a deep desire to seek You collectively. Teach us to be faithful in gathering together in prayer, supporting and encouraging each other, and lifting up our voices in unity.

May our corporate prayers be pleasing to You, a fragrant offering that reflects our shared commitment to Your will. Guide us to pray with sincerity, humility, and faith, trusting that where two or three are gathered in Your name, You are there among us. Help us to intercede for one another, our communities, and the world, knowing that our collective prayers have the power to bring about transformation and healing.

We pray for the Holy Spirit to move powerfully in our midst as we come together in prayer. Let our hearts be attuned to Your voice, and may our prayers be aligned with Your purposes. Strengthen our bonds as a community of believers, and use our corporate prayers to advance Your kingdom on earth as it is in heaven.

Thank You, Lord, for the privilege of corporate prayer and for the ways it enriches our spiritual lives. As we move forward, may we be diligent in seeking opportunities to pray together, fostering a spirit of unity and love that reflects Your heart.

In the name of Jesus Christ, our Lord and Saviour, we pray.

Amen.

Word Puzzles
THE PRACTICE OF PRAYER
CROSSWORD

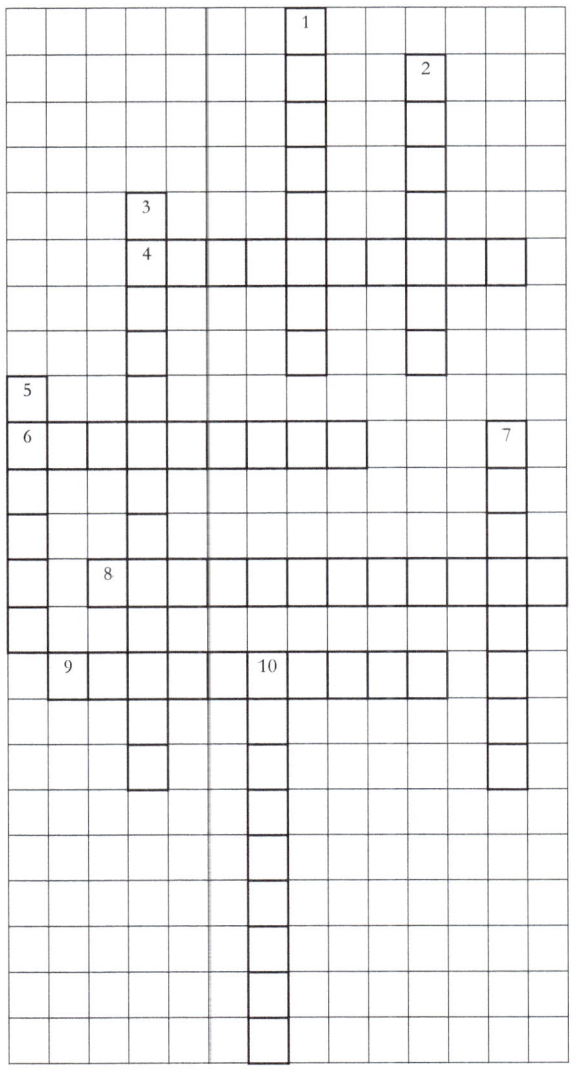

Across

4 SERIOUS THOUGHT OR CONSIDERATION

6 DEEP LOVE AND RESPECT

8 AN EARNEST PLEA

9 AN ADMISSION OF GUILT

Down

1 SHOWING DEEP AND SOLEMN RESPECT

2 A DECLARATION THAT ONE WOULD DO SOMETHING

3 A PLACE WHERE YOU RECORD YOUR CONVERSATIONS WITH GOD

5 DEDICATED TO GOD

7 RELIGIOUS WORSHIP OR OBSERVANCE

10 THE WRITINGS CONTAINED IN THE BIBLE

THE PRACTICE OF PRAYER
CROSSWORD
ANSWER

Across:
- REFLECTION
- ADORATION
- SUPPLICATION
- CONFESSION

Down:
- REVERENCE
- PROMISE
- PRAYER
- PJOURNAL (JOURNAL)
- REFLECTIONS
- INTENT
- SACRED
- DEVOTION
- CONFESSIONAL
- SCRIPTURE

Across

4 SERIOUS THOUGHT OR CONSIDERATION
6 DEEP LOVE AND RESPECT
8 AN EARNEST PLEA
9 AN ADMISSION OF GUILT

Down

1 SHOWING DEEP AND SOLEMN RESPECT
2 A DECLARATION THAT ONE WOULD DO SOMETHING
3 A PLACE WHERE YOU RECORD YOUR CONVERSATIONS WITH GOD
5 DEDICATED TO GOD
7 RELIGIOUS WORSHIP OR OBSERVANCE
10 THE WRITINGS CONTAINED IN THE BIBLE

THE PRACTICE OF PRAYER
WORDSEARCH

```
F B R T C E L F E R H N Y J H U F
P K T B F A S T I N G F Y T X E C
N F B N N I F G N C Q D J C O R G
L M E R E W C B C B S E B O O U Q
F E A T O R X U F J S V P N H T V
K V J A A N E S G I A R B F W P B
I X Z Z J L Q V M R A M Z E R I P
G Q W X M K P O E Y G M L S B R W
L S L C U E R M E R C V S S K C M
X K V C V P B R E H F P W I V S A
T B R Y E D J T K T S P M O V K S
J G A C H O Z A L A N V K N U A C
X P T E U R H E L E L O F B C E N
V R U R W W Y M C L T W C R H V U
I L N Y E W S R F L M F E P P W A
Z A B A C F R P V V N D Q S N V O
L S C E K N R E N Q M L P R N Z M
```

CONFESSION	PROMISE	SACRED
CONTEMPLATE	PSALMS	SCRIPTURE
FASTING	REFLECT	
PRAYER JOURNAL	REVERENT	

THE PRACTICE OF PRAYER
WORDSEARCH--ANSWER

	1	2	3	4	5	6	7	8	9	10	11	12	13	14	15	16	17
1	F	B	R	T	C	E	L	F	E	R	H	N	Y	J	H	U	F
2	P	K	T	B	F	A	S	T	I	N	G	F	Y	T	X	E	C
3	N	F	B	N	N	I	F	G	N	C	Q	D	J	C	O	R	G
4	L	M	E	R	E	W	D	B	C	B	S	E	B	O	O	U	Q
5	F	E	A	T	O	R	X	U	F	J	S	V	P	N	H	T	V
6	K	V	J	A	A	N	E	S	G	I	A	R	B	F	W	P	B
7	I	X	Z	Z	J	L	Q	V	M	R	A	M	Z	E	R	I	P
8	G	Q	W	X	M	K	P	O	E	Y	G	M	L	S	B	R	W
9	L	S	L	C	U	E	R	M	E	R	C	V	S	S	K	C	M
10	X	K	V	C	V	P	B	R	E	H	F	P	W	I	V	S	A
11	T	B	R	Y	E	D	J	T	K	T	S	P	M	O	V	K	S
12	J	G	A	Q	H	O	Z	A	L	A	N	V	K	N	U	A	C
13	X	P	T	E	U	R	H	E	L	E	L	O	F	B	C	E	N
14	V	R	U	R	W	W	Y	M	C	L	T	W	C	R	H	V	U
15	I	L	N	Y	E	W	S	R	F	L	M	F	E	P	P	W	A
16	Z	A	B	A	C	F	R	P	V	V	N	D	Q	S	N	V	O
17	L	S	C	E	K	N	R	E	N	Q	M	L	P	R	N	Z	M

The words below are listed with their starting row and column

CONFESSION 3:14	PROMISE 10:6	SACRED 11:17
CONTEMPLATE 14:13	PSALMS 10:12	SCRIPTURE 10:16
FASTING 2:5	REFLECT 1:10	
PRAYER JOURNAL 5:13	REVERENT 9:10	

PART IV

CHALLENGES AND GROWTH IN PRAYER

CHAPTER 16

OVERCOMING PRAYER OBSTACLES

Doubt and discouragement are two roadblocks to the power of prayer.

Opening Prayer

Heavenly Father,

As we begin this chapter on "Overcoming Prayer Obstacles," we come before You with humble hearts, seeking Your wisdom and guidance. Thank You for the gift of prayer, a precious means of communicating with You, finding solace, and seeking guidance. We acknowledge that, at times, we face challenges and barriers in our prayer lives that hinder our connection with You.

Lord, we ask for Your help as we explore the obstacles that can impede our prayers. Open our eyes to recognize these barriers and give us the courage and strength to overcome them. Help us to understand the root causes of our struggles and to find practical and spiritual solutions to deepen our prayer lives.

Lord, may Your Holy Spirit be our guide and teacher as we navigate through this chapter. Illuminate the scriptures and principles that will help us break through the obstacles we face in prayer. Encourage us to persist in prayer, even when it feels difficult or discouraging, and to trust in Your faithfulness to hear and respond.

Remove any distractions, doubts, or fears that may hinder our prayers. Grant us the discipline to cultivate a consistent and meaningful prayer life, and the perseverance to keep seeking You despite challenges. May we learn to approach You with confidence, knowing that You are always ready to listen and to help us grow.

Lord, as we journey through this chapter, may we be inspired and equipped to overcome the obstacles in our prayer lives. Let our struggles become stepping stones to a deeper, more intimate relationship with You. Fill us with a renewed sense of purpose and passion for prayer, knowing that it is through prayer that we draw closer to Your heart.

Thank You for Your patience and grace as we work to overcome these obstacles. May this chapter strengthen our commitment to a vibrant prayer life and enrich our spiritual journey in profound ways.

In the precious name of Jesus Christ, our Lord and Savior, we pray.

Amen.

Introduction

Prayer is a fundamental aspect of the Christian life, a direct line of communication with our Heavenly Father. However, many believers encounter obstacles that hinder their prayer life. These obstacles can range from doubt and unbelief to spiritual dryness, discouragement, and the challenge of unanswered prayers. Overcoming these barriers is essential for a vibrant and effective prayer life. This chapter explores these common obstacles and provides practical strategies to overcome them, ensuring that our prayers remain fervent, faithful, and fruitful.

Doubt and Unbelief

Doubt and unbelief are significant obstacles to effective prayer. They can stem from past disappointments, a lack of understanding of God's character, or the influence of a skeptical world. When we doubt, we question God's ability or willingness to answer our prayers, which can undermine our faith and hinder our prayers.

Understanding Doubt and Unbelief

Biblical Examples: The Bible provides numerous examples of individuals who struggled with doubt. For instance, Thomas doubted Jesus' resurrection:

Now Thomas (also known as Didymus), one of the Twelve, was not with the disciples when Jesus came. So the other disciples told him, "We have seen the Lord!"

But he said to them, "Unless I see the nail marks in his hands and put my finger where the nails were, and put my hand into his side, I will not believe."

A week later his disciples were in the house again, and Thomas was with them. Though the doors were locked, Jesus came and stood among them and said, "Peace be with you!" Then he said to Thomas, "Put your finger here; see my hands. Reach out your hand and put it into my side. Stop doubting and believe."

Thomas said to him, "My Lord and my God!"

Then Jesus told him, "Because you have seen me, you have believed; blessed are those who have not seen and yet have believed." **((John 20:24-29, NIV).**

Also, Peter doubted while walking on water:

"Lord, if it's you," Peter replied, *"tell me to come to you on the water."*

"Come," he said.

Then Peter got down out of the boat, walked on the water and came toward Jesus. But when he saw the wind, he was afraid and, beginning to sink, cried out, "Lord, save me!"

Immediately Jesus reached out his hand and caught him. "You of little faith," he said, "why did you doubt?" **(Matthew 14:28-31, NIV).**

Root Causes: Doubt often arises from past disappointments, fear of vulnerability, or lack of knowledge about God's promises and character.

Strategies to Overcome Doubt and Unbelief

Immerse in Scripture: Regularly read and meditate on God's Word to understand His character, promises, and faithfulness. Scriptures like the following Hebrews 11:6 and James 1:6-8 emphasize the importance of faith in prayer.

And without faith it is impossible to please God, because anyone who comes to him must believe that he exists and that he rewards those who earnestly seek him. **(Hebrews 11:6, NIV).**

But when you ask, you must believe and not doubt, because the one who doubts is like a wave of the sea, blown and tossed by the wind. That person should not expect to receive anything from the Lord. Such a person is double-minded and unstable in all they do. **(James 1:6-8, NIV).**

Recall God's Faithfulness: Reflect on past experiences where God has answered prayers and demonstrated His faithfulness. Keeping a prayer journal can help remind you of these instances.

Pray for Increased Faith: Ask God to help you overcome your unbelief, as the father in Mark 9:24 did:

"I do believe; help me overcome my unbelief!"

Seek Community Support: Share your struggles with doubt with trusted friends or mentors who can pray with you, offer encouragement, and provide perspective.

Spiritual Dryness and Discouragement

Spiritual dryness and discouragement can make prayer feel like a chore rather than a life-giving conversation with God. These periods can result from various factors, including burnout, sin, or a lack of spiritual discipline.

Understanding Spiritual Dryness

Signs of Dryness: Symptoms include a lack of desire to pray, feeling distant from God, and experiencing little joy or peace during prayer.

Root Causes: Dryness can be caused by unconfessed sin, neglecting spiritual disciplines, emotional exhaustion, or simply the ebb and flow of spiritual life.

Strategies to Overcome Spiritual Dryness and Discouragement

Confess and Repent: Identify and confess any sin that may be hindering your relationship with God. Repentance restores intimacy with Him.

Renew Spiritual Disciplines: Recommit to regular Bible reading, worship, and fellowship with other believers. These practices rekindle your passion for God.

Seek Refreshment: Spend time in nature, listen to worship music, or engage in activities that refresh your soul and draw you closer to God.

Persist in Prayer: Even when you don't feel like it, continue to pray. Ask the Holy Spirit to revive your heart and renew your passion for prayer.

Rest in God's Presence: Sometimes, simply resting in God's presence without saying a word can be refreshing. Letting go of the pressure to perform can help you reconnect with Him.

Dealing with Unanswered Prayers

God does not always hear our prayers. The Biblical evidence is given below:

"But your iniquities have separated you from your God; your sins have hidden his face from you, so that he will not hear." **(Isaiah 59:2, NIV).**

And

"Then they will call to me but I will not answer; they will look for me but will not find me." **(Proverbs 1:28, NIV).**

Even if He hears us, He may not always grant our request. His answer may be yes, no, or wait.

Unanswered prayers can be one of the most challenging obstacles to overcome. They can lead to frustration, confusion, and doubt about God's goodness and faithfulness.

Understanding Unanswered Prayers:

Biblical Examples: Even faithful individuals like Paul and Jesus experienced unanswered prayers. Notice the following:

In the case of Paul,

Therefore, in order to keep me from becoming conceited, I was given a thorn in my flesh, a messenger of Satan, to torment me. Three times I pleaded with the Lord to take it away from me. But he said to me, "My grace is sufficient for you, for my power is made perfect in weakness." Therefore I will boast all the more gladly about my weaknesses, so that Christ's power may rest on me. **(2 Corinthians 12:7-9, NIV).**

In the case of Jesus,

Going a little farther, he fell with his face to the ground and prayed, "My Father, if it is possible, may this cup be taken from me. Yet not as I will, but as you will." **(Matthew 26:39, NIV).**

Possible Reasons: Unanswered prayers can result from God's timing, His higher purposes, unconfessed sin, or praying outside of God's will.

Strategies to Deal with Unanswered Prayers

Trust in God's Sovereignty: Remember that God is sovereign and has a perfect plan. Trust that His ways are higher than our ways.

"For my thoughts are not your thoughts, neither are your ways my ways," declares the LORD. "As the heavens are higher than the earth, so are my ways higher than your ways and my thoughts than your thoughts." **(Isaiah 55:8-9, NIV).**

Seek God's Will: Align your prayers with God's will by immersing yourself in Scripture and seeking His guidance. Praying for His will to be done helps you accept His answers, even when they differ from your desires.

Examine Your Heart: Reflect on whether there are any hindrances, such as unforgiveness or selfish motives, that might be affecting your prayers.

"When you ask, you do not receive, because you ask with wrong motives, that you may spend what you get on your pleasures." **(James 4:3, NIV).**

Wait Patiently: God's timing is perfect, and sometimes the answer to our prayers is "not yet." Trust in His timing and continue to seek Him faithfully.

Find Comfort in Community: Share your struggles with unanswered prayers with your faith community. Others can offer support, encouragement, and perspective.

Conclusion

Overcoming prayer obstacles is essential for a thriving spiritual life. Doubt, unbelief, spiritual dryness, discouragement, and unanswered prayers can all hinder our communication with God. By understanding these challenges and employing practical strategies to address them, we can deepen our prayer life and grow closer to God. Remember that prayer is a journey, and obstacles are opportunities for growth and deeper reliance on God. As we persist in prayer and trust in His faithfulness, we will experience the transformative power of a vibrant and effective prayer life.

Closing Prayer

Heavenly Father,

As we conclude this chapter on "Overcoming Prayer Obstacles," we come before You with grateful hearts, thankful for the wisdom and guidance You have provided. We acknowledge that, at times, our prayer lives face challenges and obstacles that can hinder our connection with You. Yet, we are encouraged and strengthened by the understanding that You are always present, ready to help us overcome these barriers.

Lord, we ask for Your help in recognizing and addressing the obstacles that impede our prayers. Whether they be doubts, distractions, busyness, or feelings of unworthiness, we lay them all at Your feet. We pray for the Holy Spirit to work in us, removing these hindrances and filling us with a renewed passion for prayer.

Grant us perseverance and patience as we navigate through the difficulties we encounter in our prayer lives. Help us to trust in Your timing and Your ways, knowing that You are faithful to hear us and answer according to Your perfect will. Strengthen our faith, so that we may approach You with confidence and expectation.

Teach us to be resilient and steadfast in our commitment to prayer, even when we face obstacles. May we find comfort in Your presence, encouragement in Your promises, and motivation in the knowledge that prayer is a powerful and transformative practice. Help us to rely on Your strength, rather than our own, as we seek to overcome any challenges that come our way.

Lord, we thank You for Your grace and patience with us as we grow in our prayer lives. May we continually seek to deepen our relationship with You through prayer, allowing nothing to stand in the way of our communion with You. As we overcome these obstacles, may our prayers become even more fervent, sincere, and impactful.

In the name of Jesus Christ, our Lord and Saviour, we pray.

Amen.

CHAPTER 17

DEEPENING YOUR PRAYER LIFE

Praying with a partner can deepen your prayer life.

Opening Prayer

Heavenly Father,

As we begin this chapter on "Deepening Your Prayer Life," we come before You with hearts full of desire to know You more intimately and to grow closer to You through prayer. Thank You for the incredible privilege of communicating with You, for the assurance that You hear us, and for the love that draws us into deeper fellowship with You.

Lord, we ask for Your guidance and inspiration as we explore the ways to enrich and deepen our prayer lives. Open our hearts and minds to new insights and practices that will help us connect with You on a more profound level. Teach us to listen for Your voice, to seek Your presence, and to align our prayers with Your will.

We pray for the Holy Spirit to be our counselor and companion as we embark on this journey. Illuminate the scriptures and principles that will guide us into a richer and more meaningful prayer life. Encourage us to cultivate a habit of prayer that is heartfelt, sincere, and constant, knowing that through prayer, we can experience Your peace, guidance, and power.

Remove any obstacles or distractions that may hinder our growth in prayer. Grant us the discipline to make time for prayer amidst our busy lives and the perseverance to seek You earnestly. Help us to approach prayer with faith, expectancy, and a deep sense of devotion, recognizing that it is through prayer that we draw near to Your heart.

Lord, as we journey through this chapter, may we be inspired and equipped to deepen our prayer lives in ways that transform our relationship with You. Let our prayers be a reflection of our love for You and our trust in Your goodness and sovereignty. May we emerge from this chapter with a renewed passion for prayer and a deeper awareness of Your presence in our lives.

Thank You for Your endless grace and for the ways You invite us into deeper communion with You. May this chapter be a stepping stone to a vibrant and dynamic prayer life that brings glory to Your name.

In the precious name of Jesus Christ, our Lord and Savior, we pray.

Amen.

Introduction

Prayer is more than a mere ritual; it is an intimate conversation with God that deepens our relationship with Him. As we grow in our spiritual journey, it becomes essential to move beyond basic prayer practices and explore deeper, more profound ways to connect with our Creator. This chapter aims to guide you in deepening your prayer life by introducing advanced prayer techniques, contemplative and meditative prayer practices, ways to experience God's presence, and additional insights to enrich your spiritual communion.

Advanced Prayer Techniques

As you mature in your faith, exploring advanced prayer techniques can lead to a more profound and fulfilling prayer experience. These methods can help you engage with God on a deeper level and allow for more intimate communication.

Lectio Divina

Lectio Divina, or "divine reading," is an ancient practice that involves meditative reading of Scripture. It consists of four steps: reading (lectio), meditation (meditatio), prayer (oratio), and contemplation (contemplatio).

Lectio (Reading): Choose a passage of Scripture and read it slowly, allowing the words to sink in.

Meditatio (Meditation): Reflect on the passage, considering its meaning and how it speaks to your current situation.

Oratio (Prayer): Respond to the passage with a prayer, expressing your thoughts, emotions, and desires to God.

Contemplatio (Contemplation): Rest in God's presence, allowing Him to speak to your heart and mind.

The Examen

The Examen is a reflective prayer practice developed by St. Ignatius of Loyola. It involves examining your day in the presence of God, focusing on gratitude, reflection, and seeking His guidance.

Gratitude: Begin by thanking God for the blessings and experiences of the day.

Reflection: Reflect on the events of the day, considering how you responded to God's presence and guidance.

Contrition: Confess any shortcomings or failures, asking for God's forgiveness and strength to do better.

Renewal: Seek God's direction and guidance for the coming day, asking for His help to live according to His will.

Intercessory Prayer

Intercessory prayer involves praying on behalf of others. It requires a selfless heart and a deep concern for the needs and well-being of those around you.

Identify Needs: Make a list of individuals, communities, or situations that require prayer.

Pray Specifically: Pray for specific needs, asking God to intervene and provide according to His will.

Follow Up: Stay connected with those you pray for, offering support and encouragement as needed.

Contemplative and Meditative Prayer

Contemplative and meditative prayer practices focus on stillness, silence, and deep reflection, allowing for a more profound connection with God. These methods help you quiet your mind and heart, creating space for God's presence and guidance.

Centering Prayer

Centering prayer is a form of contemplative prayer that emphasizes quieting the mind and resting in God's presence.

Choose a Sacred Word: Select a word or phrase that symbolizes your intention to be in God's presence (e.g., "Jesus," "peace," "love").

Settle into Silence: Sit or kneel comfortably and close your eyes. Begin to silently repeat your sacred word, focusing on God's presence.

Return to the Word: Whenever distractions arise, gently return to your sacred word, refocusing on God.

Breath Prayer

Breath prayer involves aligning your breathing with a simple prayer phrase, creating a rhythm that helps you stay focused on God.

Choose a Phrase: Select a short prayer phrase (e.g., "Lord, have mercy," "Come, Holy Spirit").

Coordinate with Breathing: Inhale deeply while silently saying the first part of the phrase, and exhale while saying the second part.

Maintain the Rhythm: Continue this rhythmic prayer for several minutes, allowing it to center your thoughts and bring you into God's presence.

Mindfulness Meditation

Mindfulness meditation involves being fully present in the moment, focusing on God's presence and the sensations of the present time.

Find a Quiet Space: Sit or kneel comfortably in a quiet place, free from distractions.

Focus on Your Breathing: Pay attention to your breath, noticing the sensation of each inhale and exhale.

Be Present: As thoughts arise, gently acknowledge them and let them go, returning your focus to your breath and God's presence.

Experiencing God's Presence

Experiencing God's presence is the ultimate goal of deepening your prayer life. It involves cultivating an awareness of His nearness and learning to recognize His voice and guidance.

Practicing God's Presence

Inspired by Brother Lawrence's classic work, "The Practice of the Presence of God,"* this approach involves consciously acknowledging God's presence throughout your day.

Constant Awareness

Make a habit of turning your thoughts to God during everyday activities, recognizing His presence in all aspects of your life.

*https://churchleaders.com/pastors/free-resources-pastors/145403-brother-lawrence-free-ebook-the-practice-of-the-presence-of-god.html

Short Prayers: Offer short prayers and praises to God as you go about your day, inviting Him into every moment.

Mindful Living: Be mindful of how your actions and attitudes reflect your awareness of God's presence.

Worship and Adoration

Worship and adoration are powerful ways to experience God's presence, as they focus your heart and mind on His majesty and goodness.

Private Worship: Spend time in personal worship, singing, and praising God for who He is and what He has done.

Adoration Prayers: Offer prayers of adoration, expressing your love and reverence for God.

Silence and Solitude

Silence and solitude create a conducive environment for experiencing God's presence by eliminating distractions and allowing you to focus entirely on Him.

Set Aside Time: Dedicate regular time for silence and solitude, free from interruptions.

Listen for God's Voice: In the stillness, listen for God's voice, allowing Him to speak to your heart.

Other Ways to Deepen Your Prayer Life

Prayer Partners

Having a prayer partner can provide accountability, encouragement, and shared experiences in prayer. As Proverbs 27:7 tells us, "Iron sharpens iron."

Choose a Partner: Select a trusted friend or fellow believer who shares your commitment to deepening your prayer life.

Regular Meetings: Schedule regular times to pray together, share prayer requests, and support each other.

Retreats and Extended Times of Prayer

Setting aside extended periods for prayer and retreat can provide a concentrated time to focus on God and seek His guidance.

Plan a Retreat: Organize a personal or group retreat dedicated to prayer, reflection, and seeking God.

Extended Prayer Times: Incorporate extended times of prayer into your regular schedule, allowing for deeper communion with God.

Conclusion

Deepening your prayer life is a continual journey that requires intentionality, discipline, and an open heart. By exploring advanced prayer techniques, engaging in contemplative and meditative practices, and striving to experience God's presence, you can enrich your spiritual life and draw closer to God. Remember that prayer is a dynamic and evolving relationship with the Creator, and as you commit to deepening your prayer life, you will discover new depths of intimacy, guidance, and spiritual growth. May your journey in prayer lead you to a richer, more fulfilling relationship with God, transforming every aspect of your life.

Closing Prayer

Gracious and Loving Father,

As we conclude this chapter on "Deepening Your Prayer Life," we come before You with hearts filled with gratitude for the insights and encouragement You have provided. Thank You for the opportunity to learn more about drawing closer to You through prayer. We acknowledge that a deep and meaningful prayer life is a precious gift and a vital part of our relationship with You.

Lord, we ask for Your guidance and inspiration as we seek to deepen our prayer lives. Help us to prioritize time with You, to be intentional in our prayers, and to open our hearts fully to Your presence. Teach us to listen as much as we speak, to be still and know that You are God, and to find joy in the quiet moments spent with You.

May our prayers be marked by sincerity, faith, and a longing to know You more intimately. Remove any barriers that hinder our communion with You, and fill us with a fresh passion for prayer. Help us to understand the depth of Your love and to respond with hearts full of devotion and gratitude.

Lord, we ask for the Holy Spirit to guide us and intercede for us as we seek to deepen our prayer lives. Let our prayers be infused with Your wisdom and aligned with Your will. Strengthen our resolve to remain steadfast in prayer, even in times of trial and uncertainty.

As we grow in our prayer lives, may we experience the transformative power of Your presence. Let our prayers lead to personal transformation, renewed faith, and a deeper understanding of Your purpose for our lives. May our relationship with You be enriched and our hearts be continually drawn closer to Yours.

Thank You, Father, for the gift of prayer and for the privilege of deepening our connection with You. As we move forward, may our lives reflect the beauty and power of a profound prayer life, bringing glory to Your name and drawing others to Your love.

In the precious name of Jesus Christ, our Lord and Saviour, we pray.

Amen.

CHAPTER 18
SPIRITUAL WARFARE AND PRAYER

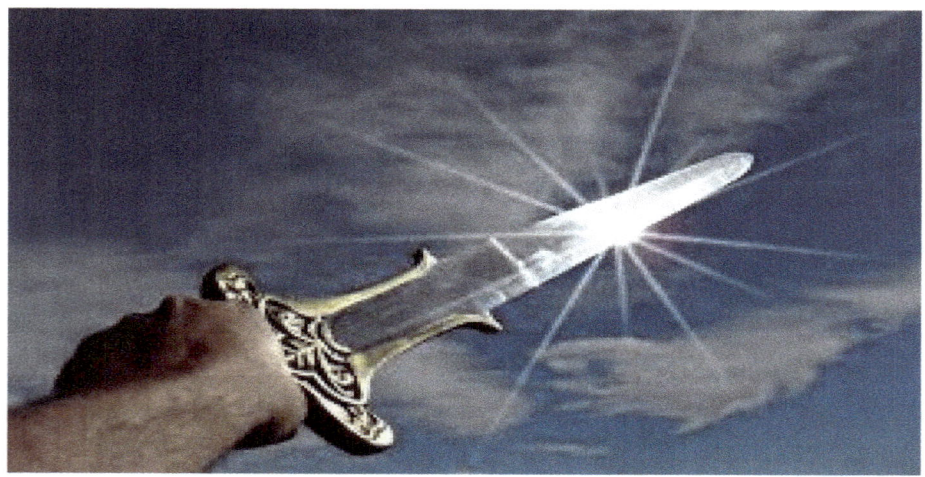

Prayer is a powerful weapon against the enemy

Opening Prayer

Mighty and Sovereign God,

As we begin this chapter on "Spiritual Warfare and Prayer," we come before You with a sense of reverence and urgency. We acknowledge the reality of the spiritual battles we face and the necessity of prayer in overcoming them. Thank You for equipping us with the powerful weapon of prayer and for Your promise to be with us in every struggle.

Lord, we ask for Your protection and wisdom as we delve into the topic of spiritual warfare. Open our eyes to understand the nature of the spiritual conflicts we encounter and the strategies of the enemy. Strengthen our faith and resolve to stand firm in Your truth and to rely on Your strength in every battle.

Let Your Holy Spirit be our guide and teacher as we navigate this crucial aspect of our spiritual lives. Illuminate the scriptures and principles that reveal the power and effectiveness of prayer in spiritual warfare. Teach us to pray with authority and confidence, knowing that in You, we have victory over every force that opposes us.

Remove any fear, doubt, or complacency that may hinder our engagement in spiritual warfare. Fill us with courage and discernment to recognize and confront the spiritual challenges we face. Help us to put on the full armor of God and to wield the sword of the Spirit with skill and precision.

Lord, as we journey through this chapter, may we be equipped and empowered to engage in spiritual warfare with prayer as our primary weapon. Let our prayers be fervent, strategic, and rooted in Your Word. May we emerge from this chapter with a deeper understanding of our authority in Christ and a renewed commitment to pray boldly and persistently.

Thank You for Your unfailing presence and for the victory we have in Jesus Christ. May this chapter strengthen our resolve to stand firm in the face of spiritual opposition and to pray without ceasing, knowing that You are our refuge and strength.

In the powerful name of Jesus Christ, our Lord and Savior, we pray.

Amen.

Introduction

Prayer is a vital weapon in the Christian's arsenal against the forces of evil. Spiritual warfare refers to the battle between good and evil, between God's kingdom and the forces of darkness. As believers, we are called to engage in this battle, standing firm in our faith and relying on the power of prayer to protect, deliver, and strengthen us. This chapter explores the nature of spiritual warfare, how to pray for protection and deliverance, and the significance of the armour of God in prayer.

Understanding Spiritual Warfare

Spiritual warfare is a reality for every believer. It is the ongoing struggle between the kingdom of God and the kingdom of Satan, and it encompasses both the seen and unseen realms. Understanding the nature of this battle is crucial for effectively engaging in it through prayer.

Biblical Basis

The Bible provides numerous references to spiritual warfare, highlighting the existence of spiritual forces of evil and the necessity of being prepared for battle.

"For our struggle is not against flesh and blood, but against the rulers, against the authorities, against the powers of this dark world and against the spiritual forces of evil in the heavenly realms." **(Ephesians 6:12).**

"Be alert and of sober mind. Your enemy the devil prowls around like a roaring lion looking for someone to devour." **(1 Peter 5:8).**

"Behold, I have given you authority to tread on serpents and scorpions, and over all the power of the enemy, and nothing shall hurt you." **(Luke 10:19).**

"No weapon that is fashioned against you shall succeed, and you shall refute every tongue that rises against you in judgment. This is the heritage of the servants of the Lord and their vindication from me, declares the Lord." **(Isaiah 54:17).**

A Spiritual Warfare Prayer

Increase my faith, Lord. Blot out my iniquities, so that I may appear spotless in your righteousness. Make me brave, so I can stand and fight the spiritual battles in my life and in our world. Give me your wisdom and discernment so I won't be caught off guard. Together, Lord, we'll win, because in truth, you already have. While evil still roams, the power of Your name and Your blood rises up to defeat and bring us victory against every evil planned against us. While malicious actions may disturb us, we use the armor of God You have given us to stand firm. You will bring justice in due time for all the harm and needless violence aimed at Your children. Until then, we remain in Your presence, aligned with Your purposes, and we look to You as our Supreme Commander and Protector. Help us to avoid temptation and deliver us from evil, Lord. You are the Mighty One, the One Who will ultimately bring all evil to light. With You, Jesus, we are safe. Amen.

Source: https://www.biblestudytools.com/topical-verses/spiritual-warfare-scriptures/

Recognizing the Enemy

The enemy in spiritual warfare is Satan and his demonic forces. They seek to undermine God's work, deceive believers, and lead people away from the truth.

Satan's Tactics: Satan uses various tactics, including deception, temptation, accusation, and fear, to attack believers.

Spiritual Discernment: It is essential to develop spiritual discernment to recognize these tactics and respond appropriately.

The Believer's Authority

As Christians, we have been given authority over the powers of darkness through Jesus Christ.

Luke 10:19: "I have given you authority to trample on snakes and scorpions and to overcome all the power of the enemy; nothing will harm you."

James 4:7: "Submit yourselves, then, to God. Resist the devil, and he will flee from you."

Praying for Protection and Deliverance

Prayer is a powerful tool for seeking God's protection and deliverance from spiritual attacks. By turning to God in prayer, we can find refuge, strength, and victory over the enemy.

Praying for Protection

Praying for protection involves asking God to shield us from the enemy's attacks and to guard our hearts, minds, and bodies.

Psalm 91: This psalm is a powerful prayer of protection, declaring God's promise to be our refuge and fortress.

Whoever dwells in the shelter of the Most High will rest in the shadow of the Almighty. I will say of the LORD, "He is my refuge and my fortress, my God, in whom I trust." Surely he will save you from the fowler's snare and from the deadly pestilence. He will cover you with his feathers, and under his wings you will find refuge; his faithfulness will be your shield and rampart. You will not fear the terror of night, nor the arrow that flies by day, nor the pestilence that stalks in the darkness, nor the plague that destroys at midday. A thousand may fall at your side, ten thousand at your right hand, but it will not come near you. You will only observe with your eyes and see the punishment of the wicked. If you say, "The LORD is my refuge," and you make the Most High your dwelling, no harm will overtake you, no disaster will come near your tent. For he will command his angels concerning you to guard you in all your ways; they will lift you up in their hands, so that you will not strike your foot against a stone. You will tread on the lion and the cobra; you will trample the great lion and the serpent. "Because he loves me," says the LORD, "I will rescue him; I will protect him, for he acknowledges my name. He will call on me, and I will answer him; I will be with him in trouble, I will deliver him and honor him. With long life I will satisfy him and show him my salvation."

Daily Prayer: Incorporate prayers for protection into your daily routine, asking God to cover you with His protective hand and to surround you with His angels.

Praying for Deliverance

When facing spiritual attacks, praying for deliverance is essential. This involves asking God to break the enemy's hold and to set us free from any bondage or oppression.

Psalm 34:17: "The righteous cry out, and the Lord hears them; he delivers them from all their troubles."

Mark 9:29: Jesus emphasized the importance of prayer in deliverance: "This kind can come out only by prayer."

Praying with Authority

Praying with authority means standing on the truth of God's Word and exercising the authority given to us through Jesus Christ.

Use Scripture: Declare God's promises and truths from the Bible as you pray for protection and deliverance.

In Jesus' Name: Pray in the name of Jesus, recognizing the power and authority that comes from His name.

The Armour of God in Prayer

The armour of God, as described in Ephesians 6:10-18, is essential for spiritual warfare. Putting on this armour through prayer equips us to stand firm against the enemy's attacks.

The Belt of Truth

Prayer Focus: Pray for a deep understanding and commitment to God's truth, asking for discernment to recognize and reject lies and deception.

The Breastplate of Righteousness

Prayer Focus: Pray for righteousness in your life, asking God to help you live in obedience and integrity, protected by His righteousness.

The Gospel of Peace

Prayer Focus: Pray for the readiness to share the gospel and for God's peace to guard your heart and mind in all circumstances.

The Shield of Faith

Prayer Focus: Pray for a strong and unwavering faith, asking God to help you trust Him fully and to extinguish the enemy's fiery darts.

The Helmet of Salvation

Prayer Focus: Pray for assurance of your salvation and protection for your mind, asking God to guard your thoughts and renew your mind.

The Sword of the Spirit

Prayer Focus: Pray for a deep understanding of God's Word, asking the Holy Spirit to help you wield it effectively in spiritual battles.

Praying in the Spirit

Prayer Focus: Pray in the Spirit at all times, seeking God's guidance, strength, and wisdom in every situation.

Conclusion

Spiritual warfare is an unavoidable reality for Christians, but we are not left defenseless. Through prayer, we can seek God's protection, deliverance, and strength to stand firm against the enemy. By understanding the nature of spiritual warfare, praying for protection and deliverance, and putting on the armour of God, we are equipped to engage in this battle victoriously. As we commit to a life of prayer, we will experience God's power and presence, enabling us to overcome the forces of darkness and live in the light of His truth.

Closing Prayer

Mighty and Sovereign God,

As we conclude this chapter on "Spiritual Warfare and Prayer," we come before You with a renewed awareness of the spiritual battles we face and the power of prayer as our greatest weapon. Thank You for equipping us with Your Word, Your Spirit, and the authority to stand firm against the forces of darkness. We are grateful for the victory we have in Christ Jesus and for the strength You provide to overcome every challenge.

Lord, we ask for Your protection and guidance as we engage in spiritual warfare. Help us to be vigilant, discerning, and courageous in the face of the enemy's schemes. Clothe us with Your full armour so that we may stand firm in the truth, righteousness, faith, salvation, and the gospel of peace. Teach us to wield the sword of the Spirit, which is Your Word, with wisdom and precision.

Strengthen our prayer lives, Lord, so that we may effectively combat the spiritual forces that seek to disrupt our lives and hinder Your work. Help us to pray with authority and confidence, knowing that You hear us and that You are faithful to act on our behalf. May our prayers be fervent and persistent, grounded in the knowledge of Your power and Your promises.

We pray for the Holy Spirit to empower us, to give us boldness and clarity as we pray against the forces of evil. Help us to intercede for ourselves, our loved ones, our communities, and the world trusting in Your mighty power to bring about change and deliverance. May we always remember that the battle belongs to You and that through Christ, we are more than conquerors.

Lord, we thank You for the assurance that You are always with us, fighting for us and protecting us. As we move forward, may we be ever mindful of the spiritual warfare around us and be diligent in prayer. Strengthen our resolve, deepen our faith, and keep us anchored in Your truth.

In the powerful name of Jesus Christ, our Lord and Saviour, we pray. Amen.

Word Puzzles

CHALLENGES AND GROWTH IN PRAYER
CROSSWORD

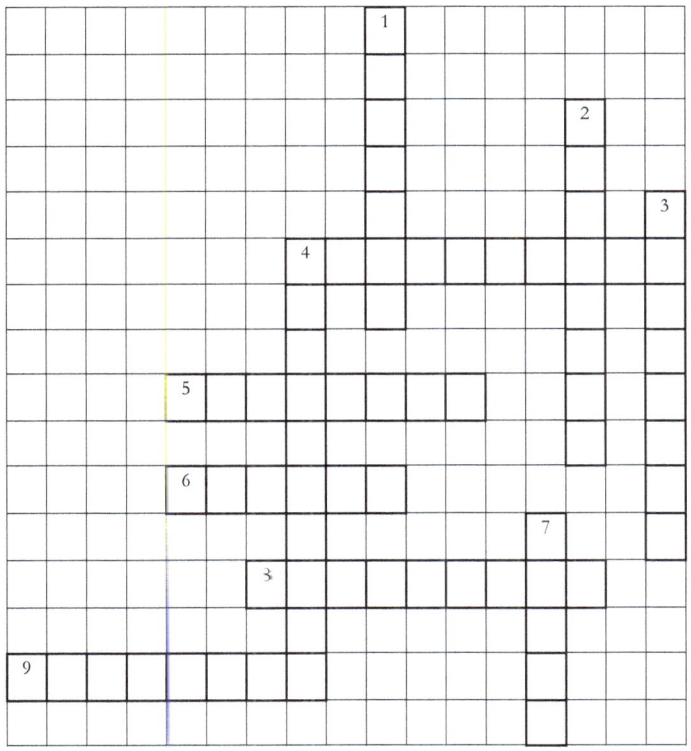

Across

4   A STATE OF FEELING PENITENT

5   REMAINING LOYAL AND STEADFAST

6   A REFLECTIVE PRAYER PRACTICE

8   DELIVERANCE FROM SIN AND ITS CONSEQUENCES

9   THE STATE OF BEING ALONE

Down

1   HAVING A PASSIONATE INTENSITY

2   PRODUCING GOOD RESULTS

3   ABSENCE OF FAITH

4   THINK DEEPLY AND AT LENGTH

7   LACK OF CONVICTION

CHALLENGES AND GROWTH IN PRAYER
CROSSWORD--ANSWER

```
                    F
                    E
                    R           F
                    V           R
                    E           U        U
                  C O N T R I T I O N
                  O   T       T        L
                  N           F        E
          F A I T H F U L     U        L
                  E           L        I
          E X A M E N                  E
                  L       D            F
              S A L V A T I O N
                  I       U
  S O L I T U D E         B
                          I
```

Across

4 A STATE OF FEELING PENITENT

5 REMAINING LOYAL AND STEADFAST

6 A REFLECTIVE PRAYER PRACTICE

8 DELIVERANCE FROM SIN AND ITS CONSEQUENCES

9 THE STATE OF BEING ALONE

Down

1 HAVING A PASSIONATE INTENSITY

2 PRODUCING GOOD RESULTS

3 ABSENCE OF FAITH

4 THINK DEEPLY AND AT LENGTH

7 LACK OF CONVICTION

CHALLENGES AND GROWTH IN PRAYER WORDSEARCH

```
P F A M C M A I H Y Q J R L
Q E Z Q S O M N E M A X E C
D K S U N T N E V R E F M M
C F A O F A I T H F U L M L
X O E G L X F I R E N A Y H
F B N I Z I F R U I T F U L
W Z O T L P T O D T T P S O
S V N R E E S U M J A I F N
C A I D D M B S D U N L O P
D O U B T Y P N V E E P N N
L P A G N M G L U M O L A C
Z F D S S A L V A T I O N G
C E H L Y I C I G T I B Z Y
R U O S N B X V P S E N Z L
```

CONTEMPLATE	FAITHFUL	SOLITUDE
CONTRITION	FERVENT	UNBELIEF
DOUBT	FRUITFUL	
EXAMEN	SALVATION	

CHALLENGES AND GROWTH IN PRAYER
WORDSEARCH---ANSWER

	1	2	3	4	5	6	7	8	9	10	11	12	13	14
1	P	F	A	M	C	M	A	I	H	Y	Q	J	R	L
2	Q	E	Z	Q	S	O	M	N	E	M	A	X	E	C
3	D	K	S	U	N	T	N	E	V	R	E	F	M	M
4	C	F	A	O	F	A	I	T	H	F	U	L	M	L
5	X	O	E	G	L	X	F	I	R	E	N	A	Y	H
6	F	B	N	I	Z	I	F	R	U	I	T	F	U	L
7	W	Z	O	T	L	P	T	O	D	T	T	P	S	O
8	S	V	N	R	E	E	S	U	M	J	A	I	F	N
9	C	A	I	D	D	M	B	S	D	U	N	L	O	P
10	D	O	U	B	T	Y	P	N	V	E	E	P	N	N
11	L	P	A	G	N	M	G	L	U	M	O	L	A	C
12	Z	F	D	S	S	A	L	V	A	T	I	O	N	G
13	C	E	H	L	Y	I	C	I	G	T	I	B	Z	Y
14	R	U	O	S	N	B	X	V	P	S	E	N	Z	L

The words below are listed with their starting row and column

    CONTEMPLATE 4:1   FAITHFUL 4:5   SOLITUDE 3:3

    CONTRITION 1:5   FERVENT 3:12   UNBELIEF 11:9

    DOUBT 10:1   FRUITFUL 6:7

    EXAMEN 2:13   SALVATION 12:5

PART V
THE IMPACT OF PRAYER

CHAPTER 19
PERSONAL TRANSFORMATION THROUGH PRAYER

Prayer leads to a complete transformation of character.

Opening Prayer

Heavenly Father,

As we begin this chapter on "Personal Transformation through Prayer," we come before You with open hearts and a deep desire for change. Thank You for the incredible gift of prayer, through which we can commune with You, seek Your guidance, and experience Your transformative power. We are grateful for Your promise to renew and shape us as we draw near to You in prayer.

Lord, we ask for Your guidance and inspiration as we explore how prayer can bring about personal transformation in our lives. Open our minds to understand the ways in which prayer can change our hearts, our thoughts, and our actions. Help us to see the areas in our lives that need Your touch and to surrender them to You.

We pray that the Holy Spirit will be our teacher and guide as we delve into this important topic. Illuminate the scriptures and principles that reveal the transformative power of prayer. Encourage us to approach prayer with faith and expectancy, knowing that through prayer, You can mold us into the image of Christ.

Remove any obstacles or doubts that may hinder our growth and transformation. Grant us the courage to be honest with ourselves and with You, and the willingness to be changed. Help us to persevere in prayer, even when the journey seems long or challenging, trusting that You are at work within us.

Lord, as we journey through this chapter, may we be inspired and equipped to embrace the transformative power of prayer. Let our prayers be marked by sincerity, humility, and a deep longing for more of You. May we emerge from this chapter with a renewed passion for prayer and a deeper awareness of Your work in our lives.

Thank You for Your endless grace and for the ways You invite us into deeper communion with You. May this chapter be a catalyst for profound personal transformation that brings glory to Your name.

In the precious name of Jesus Christ, our Lord and Saviour, we pray.

Amen.

Introduction

Prayer is not merely a spiritual exercise; it is the lifeline of a believer, a direct connection with the divine that transforms hearts and minds. This chapter explores the profound impact prayer has on personal transformation, illustrating how intimate communication with God leads to a life marked by holiness, Christlikeness, and testimonies of changed lives. Through prayer, believers find strength, guidance, and the power to overcome challenges, leading to a complete transformation of their character and actions.

Testimonies of Changed Lives

Christiana's Journey from Anxiety to Peace

Christiana, a young mother, struggled with crippling anxiety. Through persistent prayer and surrendering her fears to God, she found peace that surpassed all understanding. Her transformation was not immediate but gradual, marked by moments of divine reassurance and a growing trust in God's providence. Today, Christiana testifies of her journey, inspiring others to trust in the power of prayer to overcome mental health challenges.

Christopher's Transformation from Addiction to Freedom

Christopher battled addiction for years, feeling trapped in a cycle of despair. It was through earnest prayer and the support of a praying community that he experienced deliverance. His prayers for strength and the grace to resist temptation were answered, leading to a complete turnaround. John now leads a support group, sharing his story of hope and the transformative power of prayer.

Marlene's Healing and Forgiveness

Marlene harbored deep resentment towards her estranged father. Her journey through prayer led her to a place of healing and forgiveness. By continuously praying for the ability to forgive, she felt her heart soften and her spirit lifted. Her relationship with her father has since been restored, a testament to the healing power of prayer.

The Role of Prayer in Personal Holiness

Holiness is a state of being set apart for God, characterized by purity and moral integrity. Prayer plays a crucial role in cultivating personal holiness. Through prayer, believers confess their sins, seek God's forgiveness, and receive His cleansing grace. This process of regular confession and repentance aligns one's heart with God's will, fostering a life of holiness.

Confession and Repentance

Regular prayer involves self-examination, leading to the acknowledgment of sins and shortcomings. As believers confess their sins and repent, they experience God's forgiveness and cleansing, which is essential for personal holiness.

Seeking God's Will

Prayer aligns believers with God's will, helping them discern His guidance in their lives. This alignment is crucial for living a holy life, as it ensures that one's actions and decisions are in harmony with God's standards.

Empowerment to Overcome Temptation

Through prayer, believers receive strength to resist temptation. The Holy Spirit, invited through prayer, empowers them to overcome sinful desires and live lives that reflect God's holiness.

Growing in Christlikeness

Christlikeness is the ultimate goal of every believer, and prayer is the pathway to achieving it. Through prayer, believers cultivate a deeper relationship with Christ, allowing His character to be formed in them.

Intimacy with Christ

Prayer fosters a deep, intimate relationship with Jesus. Spending time in His presence, meditating on His words, and listening to His voice transforms believers, making them more like Christ in their thoughts, actions, and attitudes.

Fruit of the Spirit

As believers consistently pray, they open their hearts to the work of the Holy Spirit. This results in the growth of the fruit of the Spirit—love, joy, peace, patience, kindness, goodness, faithfulness, gentleness, and self-control—attributes that define Christlikeness.

Imitating Christ's Humility and Service

Prayer helps believers to understand and embrace the humility and servant-heartedness of Christ. By regularly seeking God's guidance and strength through prayer, they become more willing to serve others selflessly, reflecting Christ's humility in their daily lives.

Prayer as a Source of Strength and Guidance

Strength in Weakness

Prayer provides believers with the strength to endure trials and tribulations. When faced with life's challenges, prayer becomes a refuge where one can find comfort and encouragement. Believers often experience God's power most profoundly in their weakest moments, as they rely on His strength rather than their own.

Divine Guidance

Through prayer, believers seek and receive divine guidance for their lives. This guidance can come in various forms, such as a sense of peace about a decision, a word from Scripture, or a prompting from the Holy Spirit. By consistently seeking God's direction, believers can navigate their lives with confidence and clarity, knowing that they are following His will.

Renewed Perspective

Prayer helps to shift believers' perspectives from their problems to God's sovereignty. By focusing on God's greatness and faithfulness, believers can see their circumstances in light of His promises, which brings hope and reassurance. This renewed perspective is crucial for maintaining a positive and faith-filled outlook on life.

Conclusion

Personal transformation through prayer is a powerful testimony of God's work in the lives of believers. It encompasses the journey from brokenness to wholeness, from sin to holiness, and from self-centeredness to Christlikeness. Prayer is the catalyst that ignites this transformation, making it possible for believers to live lives that glorify God. Through the examples of changed lives, the cultivation of personal holiness, the growth in Christlikeness, and the strength and guidance received through prayer, it is evident that prayer is essential for personal transformation. As believers commit to a life of prayer, they will experience the profound and lasting change that only God can bring, leading to a deeper, more fulfilling relationship with Him.

Closing Prayer

Heavenly Father,

As we conclude this chapter on "Personal Transformation through Prayer," we are filled with gratitude for the profound truths and insights You have revealed to us. Thank You for the gift of prayer, through which we can commune with You, experience Your presence, and be transformed by Your love and power.

Lord, we recognize that true transformation comes from You. We ask that You continue to work in our hearts and lives, shaping us to be more like Christ. Help us to surrender fully to Your will, allowing Your Holy Spirit to guide and mold us. May our prayers be a reflection of our deep desire to grow in holiness and to live lives that honour You.

Teach us to approach You with humility and openness, ready to be changed by Your touch. Remove any barriers that hinder our growth, whether they be fears, doubts, or distractions. Fill us with Your peace, joy, and strength as we seek to walk in Your ways.

Lord, we pray for perseverance in our prayer lives. Help us to remain steadfast, even when we do not see immediate results. Remind us that You are always at work, even in the unseen, and that Your timing and plans are perfect. May our faith be strengthened as we trust in Your promises and rely on Your grace.

Thank You, Father, for the transformation that comes through a deep and abiding relationship with You. As we continue on this journey, may we be ever mindful of Your presence and Your power to change us from the inside out. Let our lives be a testimony to the transformative power of prayer, bringing glory to Your name.

In the name of Jesus Christ, our Lord and Savior, we pray.

Amen.

CHAPTER 20

PRAYER AND COMMUNITY TRANSFORMATION

Prayer promotes social justice and transforms communities.

Opening Prayer

Loving and Sovereign God,

As we begin this chapter on "Prayer and Community Transformation," we come before You with hearts full of hope and expectation. Thank You for the privilege of prayer and for the way it can impact not only our lives but also the lives of those around us. We are grateful for Your promise to hear our prayers and to work through them to bring about change.

Lord, we ask for Your guidance and wisdom as we explore how prayer can transform our communities. Open our eyes to see the needs and challenges facing our neighbourhoods, cities, and nations. Help us to understand how we can be instruments of Your love and peace through our prayers.

Father, let Your Holy Spirit be our teacher and guide as we delve into this vital topic. Illuminate the scriptures and examples that show the power of prayer in community transformation. Inspire us with stories of how You have moved in communities through the prayers of Your people, and stir in us a passion to intercede for those around us.

Remove any apathy or discouragement that may hinder our commitment to pray for our communities. Fill us with compassion for the lost, the hurting, and the oppressed. Grant us the faith to believe that our prayers can make a difference and the perseverance to continue praying even when we do not see immediate results.

Lord, as we journey through this chapter, may we be inspired and equipped to become fervent prayer warriors for our communities. Let our prayers be marked by love, humility, and a deep sense of partnership with You in Your redemptive work. May we see transformation in our communities as a result of our faithful prayers, and may Your kingdom come and Your will be done on earth as it is in heaven.

Thank You for the opportunity to partner with You in prayer for the sake of our communities. May this chapter ignite a passion within us to pray without ceasing and to seek Your face for the transformation of the world around us.

In the powerful name of Jesus Christ, our Lord and Saviour, we pray.

Amen.

Introduction

Prayer is a transformative force that not only impacts individual lives but also has the power to effect significant change within entire communities. When believers unite in prayer, seeking God's intervention and guidance, they can witness remarkable shifts in the spiritual, social, and cultural fabric of their surroundings. This chapter delves into the pivotal role prayer plays in community transformation, examining historical revivals, prayer movements, the practice of praying for one's community, and the influence of prayer on social justice. By understanding the collective power of prayer, believers can be inspired to engage more deeply in intercessory prayer for their communities, fostering unity, hope, and positive change.

Historical Revivals and Prayer Movements

Throughout history, there have been numerous revivals and prayer movements that have profoundly impacted communities and nations. These events serve as powerful reminders of how united prayer can lead to widespread spiritual renewal and societal transformation.

The Great Awakening (1730s-1740s)

The Great Awakening was a series of religious revivals that swept through the American colonies, characterized by fervent prayer, passionate preaching, and mass conversions. Leaders like Jonathan Edwards (1703-1758) and George Whitefield (1714-1770) emphasized the importance of prayer and repentance, which led to a significant increase in church attendance and a renewed commitment to Christian values.

The Welsh Revival (1904-1905)

The Welsh Revival, led by Evan Roberts (1878-1951), saw an extraordinary outpouring of the Holy Spirit in Wales. This revival was marked by intense prayer meetings, spontaneous worship, and a deep conviction of sin. As a result, thousands of people turned to Christ, and the revival's impact extended to social reforms, including the reduction of crime and the closure of taverns.

The Azusa Street Revival (1906-1915)

The Azusa Street Revival, led by William J. Seymour (1870-1922) in Los Angeles, is considered the birthplace of the modern Pentecostal movement. The revival was characterized by fervent prayer, speaking in tongues, and miraculous healings. It attracted a diverse group of people from various racial and socioeconomic backgrounds, breaking down barriers and fostering a sense of unity within the body of Christ.

The Jesus Movement (1960s-1970s)

The Jesus Movement emerged during the countercultural era in the United States, with young people seeking spiritual truth and authenticity. Prayer played a central role in this movement, as believers gathered in homes, parks, and beaches to pray and worship together. The movement led to a renewed emphasis on personal relationship with Jesus, evangelism, and social activism.

Praying for Your Community

Praying for one's community is a vital aspect of intercessory prayer that can lead to profound transformation. Believers are called to stand in the gap for their communities, seeking God's intervention and blessing.

Identifying Community Needs

The first step in praying for a community is to identify its specific needs. This may involve conducting research, talking to community leaders, and discerning the areas that require God's intervention, such as crime, poverty, addiction, or broken relationships.

Organizing Prayer Walks

Prayer walks involve physically walking through the community while praying for its needs. This practice allows believers to gain a deeper understanding of their surroundings and to intercede on-site for specific issues. It also provides an opportunity to connect with and minister to community members.

Establishing Prayer Groups

Forming prayer groups dedicated to praying for the community can create a sense of unity and purpose among believers. These groups can meet regularly to pray for specific needs, share testimonies of answered prayers, and encourage one another.

Engaging in Fasting and Prayer

Fasting and prayer are powerful spiritual disciplines that can intensify intercession for a community. By denying oneself of physical sustenance, believers can focus more intently on seeking God's will and intervention for their community.

Prayer's Role in Social Justice

Prayer and social justice are intricately connected, as prayer can inspire and empower believers to address systemic injustices and advocate for change.

Biblical Basis for Social Justice

The Bible is replete with calls for justice and righteousness. The following are some examples:

"He has shown you, O mortal, what is good. And what does the LORD require of you? To act justly and to love mercy and to walk humbly with your God." **(Micah 6:8).**

"Learn to do good; Seek justice, Reprove the ruthless, Defend the orphan, Plead for the widow." **(Isaiah 1:17).**

"Open your mouth, judge righteously, And defend the rights of the afflicted and needy." **(Proverbs 31:9)**

"Thus has the Lord of hosts said, 'Dispense true justice and practice kindness and compassion each to his brother; and do not oppress the widow or the orphan, the stranger or the poor; and do not devise evil in your hearts against one another." **(Zechariah 7:9-10).**

"Thus says the Lord, "Do justice and righteousness, and deliver the one who has been robbed from the power of his oppressor. Also do not mistreat or do violence to the stranger, the orphan, or the widow; and do not shed innocent blood in this place." **(Jeremiah 22:3).**

"You shall not pervert the justice due an alien or an orphan, nor take a widow's garment in pledge." **(Deuteronomy 24:17).**

"Vindicate the weak and fatherless; Do justice to the afflicted and destitute." **(Psalm 82:3).**

These verses highlight God's heart for justice and mercy. Prayer helps believers align their hearts with God's and seek His guidance in pursuing justice.

Interceding for the Oppressed

Praying for those who are marginalized, oppressed, and suffering is a crucial aspect of social justice. Believers can intercede for victims of human trafficking, racial discrimination, poverty, and other forms of injustice, asking God to bring relief, restoration, and justice.

Empowering Advocacy and Action

Prayer can inspire believers to take practical steps toward social justice. As they pray, they may receive divine direction on how to get involved, whether through volunteering, supporting relevant organizations, or advocating for policy changes. Prayer also sustains and strengthens believers as they engage in the often challenging work of social justice.

Healing and Reconciliation

Prayer plays a significant role in healing and reconciliation within communities. By praying for forgiveness, understanding, and unity, believers can contribute to the healing of historical wounds and the reconciliation of divided groups.

Other Considerations

Prayer and Community Health

Prayer can have a positive impact on the physical and mental health of a community. Studies have shown that communities with strong spiritual foundations often experience lower levels of stress, depression, and substance abuse. By praying for health and well-being, believers can contribute to the overall wellness of their community.

"if my people, who are called by my name, will humble themselves and pray and seek my face and turn from their wicked ways, then I will hear from heaven, and I will forgive their sin and will heal their land." **(2 Chronicles 7:14, NIV).**

Prayer for Education

Praying for schools, teachers, and students is vital for fostering an environment conducive to learning and growth. Believers can pray for wisdom and guidance for educators, safety and protection for students, and resources for schools to provide quality education.

Prayer for Law-enforcement Officers

Praying for law-enforcement officers is crucial for maintaining law and order in any community. The following is a prayer for law-enforcement officers:

"Most kind and ever-loving Father,

We come before You with grateful hearts for the men and women who serve as law enforcement officers. We thank You for their courage, dedication, and commitment to maintaining peace and order in our communities. Lord, we ask that You surround them with Your divine protection as they carry out their duties. Shield them from harm and danger, and grant them wisdom, discernment, and patience in every situation they encounter.

Bless them with strength and resilience to face the challenges and uncertainties of their profession. May they act with integrity, justice, and compassion, reflecting Your love and righteousness in all they do. Comfort their families who support them through the stresses and demands of their service, and give them peace and assurance.

Lord, we pray for unity and understanding between law enforcement and the communities they serve. Help us all to work together for the common good, fostering trust, respect, and cooperation. We ask that You heal any wounds of division and bring about reconciliation where there is strife.

In moments of trial and difficulty, remind our officers of Your presence and Your promises. May they find solace in Your unfailing love and strength in Your mighty power. Guide them to make decisions that honour You and uphold justice.

We lift this prayer in the name of Jesus Christ, our Saviour and Protector.

Amen."

Economic Transformation

Prayer can also influence the economic conditions of a community. By praying for economic opportunities, job creation, and ethical business practices, believers can contribute to the economic flourishing of their community. They can also seek God's guidance in addressing issues like unemployment and financial instability.

Conclusion

The transformative power of prayer extends beyond individual lives to encompass entire communities. By examining historical revivals and prayer movements, believers can be inspired by the profound impact of united prayer. Praying for one's community involves identifying its specific needs, organizing prayer walks, establishing prayer groups, and engaging in fasting and prayer. Prayer also plays a crucial role in social justice, empowering believers to advocate for change and seek healing and reconciliation. Additionally, prayer can positively influence community health, education, law enforcement, and economic conditions. As believers commit to praying for their communities, they will witness the remarkable ways in which God intervenes, bringing about lasting transformation and fostering a sense of unity, hope, and positive change.

Closing Prayer

Loving and Sovereign God,

As we conclude this chapter on "Prayer and Community Transformation," we are deeply thankful for the ways You have opened our eyes to the power of collective prayer. We acknowledge that through prayer, You work mightily not only in our individual lives but also within our communities, bringing healing, unity, and renewal.

Lord, we lift up our communities to You, asking for Your divine intervention and guidance. Teach us to pray fervently and faithfully for our neighbourhoods, cities, and nations. Help us to see the needs around us with Your eyes of compassion and to respond with prayers that are bold and aligned with Your will.

May our prayers spark transformation in our communities, breaking down barriers, fostering reconciliation, and promoting justice and peace. Empower us to be agents of change, shining Your light in dark places and spreading Your love wherever we go. Unite us as believers, strengthening our bonds as we come together in prayer and action.

We ask for the Holy Spirit to move powerfully within our communities, bringing revival and drawing hearts to You. Let our collective prayers be a testament to Your greatness and Your desire to bring about Your kingdom here on earth. Fill us with a sense of purpose and urgency, knowing that our prayers can make a difference and that You are faithful to respond.

Thank You, Lord, for the privilege of partnering with You in the work of community transformation through prayer. As we go forward, may we be ever more committed to praying for and serving our communities, trusting in Your power to bring about lasting change.

In the name of Jesus Christ, our Lord and Saviour, we pray.

Amen.

CHAPTER 21
GLOBAL IMPACT OF PRAYER

Prayer can ignite worldwide revivals.

Opening Prayer

Almighty and Sovereign God,

As we begin this final chapter on the "Global Impact of Prayer," we come before You with hearts full of awe and reverence for Your mighty power and boundless love. Thank You for the privilege of prayer and for the way it connects us to Your heart and to the needs of the world. We are grateful for the opportunity to reflect on how our prayers can transcend borders and bring about change on a global scale.

Lord, we ask for Your guidance and insight as we explore the vast and profound impact that prayer can have across nations and cultures. Open our hearts to understand the significance of interceding for the world and the ways in which You invite us to participate in Your redemptive work through prayer. Help us to see beyond our immediate surroundings and to grasp the global vision You have for Your kingdom.

May the Holy Spirit be our teacher and guide as we delve into this important topic. Illuminate the scriptures and testimonies that reveal the transformative power of prayer on a global scale. Inspire us with stories of how You have moved mightily in response to the prayers of Your people and fill us with a renewed passion to intercede for the nations.

Remove any barriers of indifference, fear, or doubt that may hinder our commitment to global prayer. Grant us a heart of compassion for the lost, the suffering, and the oppressed around the world. Equip us with the faith to believe that our prayers can make a difference and the perseverance to continue praying fervently.

Lord, as we journey through this final chapter, may we be inspired and equipped to embrace the call to global intercession. Let our prayers be marked by a deep sense of urgency, humility, and love. May we witness the ripple effects of our prayers as they bring about transformation, healing, and hope in the farthest corners of the earth.

Thank You for the incredible privilege of partnering with You in prayer for the sake of the world. May this chapter ignite a lasting commitment within us to pray without ceasing and to seek Your will for the nations. May Your kingdom come and Your will be done on earth as it is in heaven.

In the powerful name of Jesus Christ, our Lord and Savior, we pray.

Amen.

Introduction

The power of prayer transcends personal and local boundaries, reaching into the very fabric of nations and the global community. As believers, we are called to pray not only for ourselves and our immediate surroundings but also for the broader world. This chapter explores the profound global impact of prayer, demonstrating how intercession can influence nations, support missionaries, and shape the future of prayer movements. By examining historical and contemporary examples, we will see how the fervent prayers of the faithful have brought about significant change and how we can continue to harness this power for global transformation.

Praying for the Nations

Prayer for our nation is a vital aspect of intercessory prayer. The Bible commands us to pray for those in authority and for the well-being of our countries

"I urge, then, first of all, that petitions, prayers, intercession and thanksgiving be made for all people—for kings and all those in authority, that we may live peaceful and quiet lives in all godliness and holiness." **(1 Timothy 2:1-2, NIV).**

When believers unite in prayer for their nation, they invite God's guidance, wisdom, and protection over its leaders and citizens.

Praying for Leaders

Praying for national leaders, including presidents, prime ministers, and legislators, is crucial. These individuals make decisions that affect millions of lives, and they need divine wisdom, integrity, and courage to govern justly. By lifting them up in prayer, we ask God to guide their actions and decisions, aligning them with His will.

Praying for Peace and Justice

Interceding for peace and justice within a nation is essential for creating a stable and prosperous society. Believers can pray for an end to conflict, for the protection of human rights, and for the establishment of just and fair systems. Prayer can also support efforts to combat corruption, inequality, and other social injustices.

Praying for Revival

Spiritual revival can transform a nation from the inside out. By praying for a widespread awakening to God's presence and truth, believers can ignite a fire of faith that spreads throughout the country. Historical revivals have shown that when people turn to God in repentance and faith, societal changes follow, leading to moral and ethical renewal.

Missionary Stories and Prayer

The relationship between missionaries and prayer is a testament to the power of intercession in advancing the gospel worldwide. Missionaries often face immense challenges, including cultural barriers, opposition, and personal sacrifices. Prayer sustains them, opens doors, and brings about miraculous breakthroughs.

Hudson Taylor and the China Inland Mission

Hudson Taylor (1832-1905), the founder of the China Inland Mission, attributed much of his success to the fervent prayers of supporters back home. Despite the enormous difficulties he faced, including illness and opposition, prayer enabled him to establish a lasting ministry that brought countless Chinese people to Christ.

William Carey and the Power of Prayer

Known as the "father of modern missions," William Carey (1761-1834) relied heavily on prayer throughout his missionary work in India. His dedication to prayer and his belief in its power to transform lives led to significant advancements in education, social reform, and the spread of the gospel in India.

Contemporary Missionary Testimonies

Modern missionaries continue to experience the power of prayer in their ministries. Stories abound of doors opening in closed countries, protection in dangerous situations, and communities being transformed through the gospel, all as a result of persistent prayer.

The Future of Global Prayer Movements

As we look to the future, the global prayer movement holds immense potential for continued impact. Technology, increased connectivity, and a growing awareness of global issues have created unprecedented opportunities for believers to unite in prayer like never before.

Technology and Prayer

Advances in technology have made it possible for believers around the world to connect and pray together in real time. Online prayer groups, virtual prayer meetings, and social media platforms provide avenues for collective intercession, breaking down geographical barriers and fostering a sense of global unity.

Youth and Prayer Movements

The younger generation is increasingly taking up the mantle of prayer, spearheading movements that emphasize intercession for global issues such as human trafficking, poverty, and environmental stewardship. These young prayer warriors are harnessing their passion and creativity to mobilize others and effect change on a global scale.

Prayer Networks and Alliances: Organizations and networks dedicated to global prayer are growing, bringing together believers from diverse backgrounds to pray for specific needs and regions. These alliances amplify the power of prayer, creating a concerted effort to address global challenges and advance God's kingdom on earth.

Conclusion

The global impact of prayer is a testament to the boundless power of intercession. Throughout history, prayer has influenced nations, supported missionaries, and sparked movements that have shaped the world. As believers, we are called to continue this legacy, interceding for our nations, supporting those on the frontlines of mission work, and participating in global prayer movements.

In the face of a rapidly changing world, the need for prayer is more urgent than ever. By uniting in prayer, we can address the pressing issues of our time, from social injustices to spiritual darkness, and bring about God's transformative power on a global scale. As we commit to a life of prayer, we participate in the unfolding of God's plan for the world, witnessing His glory and experiencing the profound impact of His love and grace.

May we be inspired to pray without ceasing, believing in the power of prayer to change not only our lives but the world around us. Let us join hands and hearts in a global chorus of prayer, lifting our voices to heaven and trusting that God, in His infinite wisdom and mercy, will hear and answer, bringing about a new era of spiritual awakening and global transformation.

Closing Prayer

Heavenly Father,

As we conclude this chapter on the "Global Impact of Prayer," we stand in awe of Your boundless love and power that transcends all borders and nations. Thank You for the incredible privilege of coming before You in prayer, knowing that our petitions, praises, and intercessions can impact the world in profound ways.

Lord, we are grateful for the testimonies and stories of how prayer has moved mountains, transformed lives, and brought about change in the farthest corners of the earth. Help us to remain steadfast and fervent in our prayers, believing in Your ability to do immeasurably more than all we ask or imagine.

We lift up the nations to You, asking for Your guidance, peace, and justice to prevail. Teach us to pray with hearts full of compassion and hope for people we may never meet, knowing that in Your kingdom, we are all connected. Empower us to be intercessors who stand in the gap for the lost, the suffering, and the oppressed.

Guide our prayers and align them with Your heart. Break our hearts for what breaks Yours, and fill us with a relentless desire to see Your will be done on earth as it is in heaven. Let our prayers be a force for good, ushering in Your light into the darkest places and Your love into the most broken situations.

We ask for a global awakening, a revival that only You can bring. Stir the hearts of believers around the world to rise up in unified prayer, seeking Your face and calling upon Your name. May our collective prayers spark a movement that brings healing, reconciliation, and salvation to countless lives.

Thank You, Lord, for the power of prayer and for the assurance that You hear us and act on our behalf. As we move forward, may we be diligent in lifting up our world to You, trusting in Your sovereignty and Your infinite grace.

In the mighty name of Jesus Christ, our Lord and Saviour, we pray.

Amen.

CHAPTER 22

PRAYER IN HEAVEN

Eye has not seen nor ear heard....

Opening Prayer

Heavenly Father,

As we embark on this journey to explore the nature of prayer in Heaven, we seek Your divine wisdom and guidance. Open our hearts and minds to the truths revealed in Your Word. May our understanding be deepened and our spirits uplifted as we contemplate the eternal realities of Your heavenly kingdom. Fill us with awe and reverence as we consider the majesty of Your presence and the ceaseless worship that takes place before Your throne.

In Jesus' name, we pray,

Amen.

Introduction

One of the tenets of the Christian faith is that Jesus will return to take His faithful followers home where they will spend the ceaseless ages of eternity with Him. In this final chapter, we explore some crucial issues about prayer in Heaven. First, we examine the issue of the reality of heaven, then we turn our attention to scripture for insight on the topic. If there is prayer in heaven, what is the nature of the prayers? We explore this question. Finally, we end the chapter by looking at prayer as eternal worship.

Is Heaven Real?

The reality of Heaven is a fundamental tenet of the Christian faith. Throughout the Bible, Heaven is depicted as the eternal dwelling place of God, the angels, and the redeemed. Jesus Himself spoke of Heaven, providing assurance of its existence and promising a place for His followers.

"In my Father's house are many rooms. If it were not so, would I have told you that I go to prepare a place for you? And if I go and prepare a place for you, I will come again and will take you to myself, that where I am you may be also." **(John 14:2-3).**

Biblical Evidence about Prayer in Heaven

The Bible offers glimpses into the nature of prayer and worship in Heaven. Revelation, the final book of the New Testament, provides some of the most vivid descriptions. In Revelation, we see the prayers of the saints symbolized as golden bowls of incense:

"And when he had taken it, the four living creatures and the twenty-four elders fell down before the Lamb. Each one had a harp and they were holding golden bowls full of incense, which are the prayers of God's people." **(Revelations 5:8).**

This imagery suggests that the prayers of believers on earth are precious and continue to have significance in Heaven. The prayers are not forgotten but are presented before God as a fragrant offering.

And in Romans, Paul assures us that there is prayer in heaven:

Who then is the one who condemns? No one. Christ Jesus who died—more than that, who was raised to life—is at the right hand of God and is also interceding for us. **(Romans 8:34, NIV).**

Kinds of Prayer in Heaven

Now we know that there is prayer in heaven; but what is the nature of the prayers? We answer that question in this section. The nature of prayer in Heaven will likely be different from what we experience on earth. On earth, prayer often involves petitions, intercessions, and supplications, as we bring our needs and the needs of others before God. In Heaven, where there will be no more pain, sorrow, or need, prayer will transform into pure worship, adoration, and thanksgiving.

Revelation 7:9-12 describes a great multitude standing before the throne and before the Lamb, crying out with a loud voice: "Salvation belongs to our God who sits on the throne, and to the Lamb!" The angels, elders, and living creatures join in, worshipping God and proclaiming His glory and wisdom, thanksgiving, honour, power, and might.

This scene indicates that prayer in Heaven will be characterized by continuous praise and worship, a joyful and eternal acknowledgment of God's sovereignty and goodness.

Prayer as Eternal Worship

In Heaven, prayer will transcend the earthly concept of communication with God and will become an integral part of our eternal worship. The focus will shift from seeking God's help in our daily struggles to exalting Him for His eternal attributes and mighty deeds.

The book of Revelation provides a powerful image of this eternal worship. Revelation 4:8-11 describes the four living creatures and the twenty-four elders who "never cease to say, 'Holy, holy, holy, is the Lord God Almighty, who was and is and is to come!' And whenever the living creatures give glory and honour and thanks to him who is seated on the throne, who lives forever and ever, the twenty-four elders fall down before him who is seated on the throne and worship him who lives forever and ever. They cast their crowns before the throne, saying, 'Worthy are you, our Lord and God, to receive glory and honour and power, for you created all things, and by your will they existed and were created.'"

This passage illustrates the unending adoration and reverence that will define our heavenly existence. Our prayers will be expressions of worship, filled with awe and gratitude for God's eternal majesty and the salvation He has provided.

Conclusion

In conclusion, the reality of Heaven as described in the Bible assures us of a place where prayer transforms into eternal worship. The prayers of the saints on earth continue to hold significance in Heaven, symbolized by golden bowls of incense. While the nature of prayer will change, shifting from petitions to pure adoration, the essence remains: a profound connection with our Creator, characterized by worship, thanksgiving, and reverence.

May we live our lives on earth in anticipation of this glorious future, continually offering our prayers as fragrant incense before God, and looking forward to the day when our prayers will join the eternal chorus of worship in Heaven.

Closing Prayer

Heavenly Father,

As we conclude this chapter, we thank You for the insights into the nature of prayer in Heaven. Fill our hearts with a longing for Your presence and a deeper desire to worship You both now and for all eternity. Help us to live each day with the assurance of Heaven, continually lifting our prayers to You in faith and reverence. May our lives be a testament to Your glory, and may our prayers on earth echo the eternal worship that awaits us in Heaven.

In Jesus' name, we pray,

Amen.

CONCLUDING REMARKS

Introduction

As we draw to a close in our exploration of "The Power of Prayer," we reflect on the journey we've undertaken together. Throughout this book, we have delved into the transformative nature of prayer, examining its profound impact on individual lives, communities, and the world at large. Prayer is not just a religious practice but a powerful connection to the divine, a means through which we experience God's presence, guidance, and intervention in our daily lives. In these concluding remarks, we will recapitulate the key points we've covered, reaffirm the ongoing call to prayer, offer encouragement for the journey ahead, and leave you with a final word to inspire your continued growth in this vital spiritual discipline.

Recapitulation of Key Points

The Essence of Prayer

Prayer is a dynamic conversation with God, rooted in faith and trust. It involves adoration, confession, thanksgiving, and supplication, encompassing every aspect of our relationship with God.

Personal Transformation through Prayer

We explored how prayer transforms our hearts, minds, and lives. Through regular communion with God, we experience personal holiness, grow in Christlikeness, and find strength and guidance for life's challenges.

Prayer and Community Transformation

Prayer has the power to impact entire communities. Historical revivals, prayer movements, and intercessory prayers for our neighbourhoods, cities, and nations illustrate the collective power of prayer to bring about societal change.

Global Impact of Prayer

Our prayers reach beyond local borders, influencing nations and supporting missionaries worldwide. We discussed the significant role of prayer in global missions and the future potential of global prayer movements to address pressing issues and advance God's kingdom.

Practical Aspects of Prayer

Throughout the book, we provided practical guidance on how to cultivate a vibrant prayer life. This included setting aside dedicated time for prayer, using Scripture as a foundation, and incorporating various forms of prayer such as contemplative prayer, prayer walks, and corporate prayer gatherings.

The Ongoing Call to Prayer

As we conclude this book, it is essential to recognize that the call to prayer is ongoing. Prayer is not a one-time event or a sporadic activity; it is a lifelong commitment and a continuous journey of drawing closer to God. We are encouraged to "pray without ceasing" (1 Thessalonians 5:17), to make prayer an integral part of our daily lives. This ongoing call to prayer invites us to deepen our relationship with God, to intercede for others, and to remain vigilant in seeking His will and purposes in all things.

Encouragement for the Journey Ahead

The journey of prayer is both rewarding and challenging. There will be times of profound intimacy with God, moments of answered prayers, and seasons of spiritual growth. However, there will also be times of dryness, unanswered questions, and spiritual battles. It is in these moments that perseverance and faith are crucial.

Perseverance

Keep pressing on in prayer, even when it feels difficult or when answers seem delayed. God honours our persistence and faithfulness.

Faith

Trust that God hears your prayers and is working all things for our good, even when we cannot see it. Our prayers are powerful and effective, not because of our own strength, but because of God's power and love.

Community

Engage with a community of believers who can support, encourage, and pray with you. Corporate prayer and mutual encouragement are vital for sustaining a vibrant prayer life.

Growth

Continue to grow in your understanding and practice of prayer. Read books, attend seminars, join prayer groups, and seek out mentors who can guide you in your prayer journey.

Conclusion

As we close this book, we leave you with a charge and a blessing. Embrace the power of prayer in your life. Let it be the foundation upon which you build your relationship with God, the force that drives your personal and communal transformation, and the means through which you contribute to global change. Remember that prayer is not just a practice; it is a lifeline to the Creator, a source of strength, and a channel of His grace and love.

May you be inspired to pray with boldness, faith, and perseverance. May your prayers ascend as sweet incense before the Lord, bringing about His will on earth as it is in heaven. And may you experience the fullness of His presence, the joy of His fellowship, and the power of His answers to your prayers.

In all things, to God be the glory.

Closing Prayer

Heavenly Father, our Creator and Redeemer,

We come before You with hearts full of gratitude for the journey we have undertaken through the pages of this book, "The Power of Prayer: A Christian Manifesto." Thank You for the insights, revelations, and encouragement You have imparted to us as we have explored the profound impact of prayer in our lives and in the world around us.

Lord, we ask that You seal these teachings in our hearts. Help us to remember the power and privilege of prayer, and to approach Your throne of grace with confidence, knowing that You hear us and are faithful to respond. May our lives be marked by fervent, consistent, and humble prayer, seeking Your will and aligning our hearts with Yours.

As we move forward, empower us to be instruments of Your peace and love, interceding for our families, our communities, our nations, and our world. Fill us with Your Spirit, so that our prayers are infused with Your wisdom, compassion, and strength. May our prayers bring about transformation, healing, and renewal, both within us and in the world we touch.

We lift up those who read this book, asking that You guide each one into a deeper, more intimate relationship with You. Ignite within us a passion for prayer that cannot be extinguished, and use us to advance Your kingdom on earth as it is in heaven.

In all things, may Your name be glorified. We surrender our plans, desires, and lives into Your hands, trusting in Your perfect plan and timing.

We pray all this in the mighty and precious name of Jesus Christ, our Lord and Saviour.

Amen.

Word Puzzles
THE IMPACT OF PRAYER
CROSSWORD

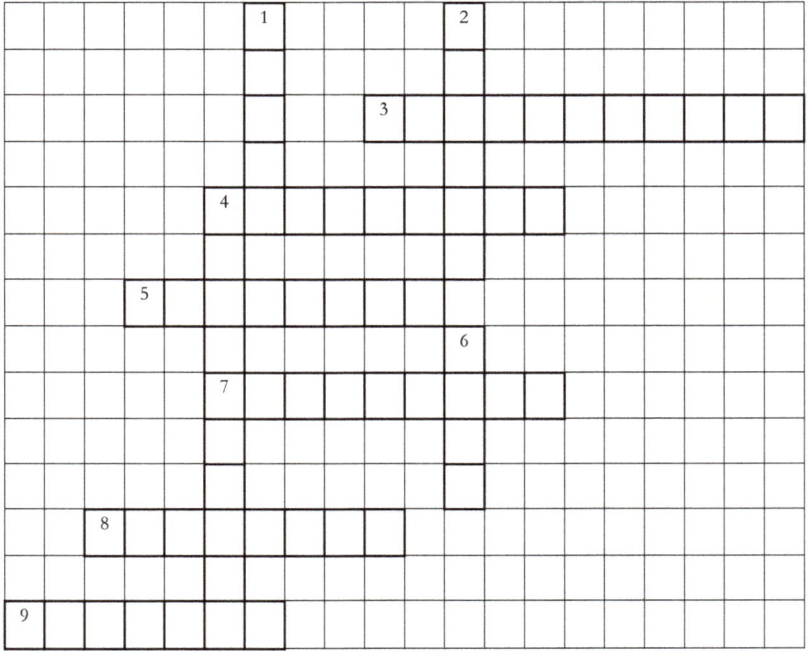

Across

3 PARDON

4 EVIDENCE OR PROOF OF SOMETHING

5 ABSENCE OF ARROGANCE

7 CHANGE THE CHARACTER OR FUNCTION OF SOMEONE

8 SOMEONE WITH RELIGIOUS FAITH

9 THE PROCESS OF BECOMING WELL OR HEALTHY

Down

1 FREEDOM FROM DISTURBANCE

2 A TALK ON A RELIGIOUS SUBJECT

4 AN ENTICEMENT TO DISOBEY GOD

6 A FEELING OF EXPECTATION OR DESIRE

THE IMPACT OF PRAYER
CROSSWORD--ANSWER

				P			S						
				E			E						
				A		F	O	R	G	I	V	E	N	E	S	S
				C			M						
			T	E	S	T	I	M	O	N	Y		
				E					N				
		H	U	M	I	L	I	T	Y				
				P					H				
			T	R	A	N	S	F	O	R	M		
				A					P				
				T					E				
		B	E	L	I	E	V	E	R				
				O									
H	E	A	L	I	N	G							

Across

3 PARDON
4 EVIDENCE OR PROOF OF SOMETHING
5 ABSENCE OF ARROGANCE
7 CHANGE THE CHARACTER OR FUNCTION OF SOMEONE
8 SOMEONE WITH RELIGIOUS FAITH
9 THE PROCESS OF BECOMING WELL OR HEALTHY

Down

1 FREEDOM FROM DISTURBANCE
2 A TALK ON A RELIGIOUS SUBJECT
4 AN ENTICEMENT TO DISOBEY GOD
6 A FEELING OF EXPECTATION OR DESIRE

THE IMPACT OF PRAYER
WORDSEARCH

```
H U M I L I T Y T S V R X T C Q U
D I T M B P E E D R E F P Q Y X C
R I X S P I P S C P P A H N D K E
R O X I S X W Y Y A W J O P S T U
R O A H S A H H V Q E M Y H R X N
R B F E E Q O W J M I P C A J Q U
N I U A N C A Q A T J I N A C R T
J B K L E W Q R S P X S C N N F A
G L L I V C V E O A F E O W L J L
X W G N I I T J W O F I N P L Z B
X S M G G M Z E R W T B O C R E M
C N X D R T M M P A H O P E L M U
U V E Y O Z A J T G V H F I A E J
T F U V F T Q P L T C S E B F H K
K Y Z V I R M J U A W V I N R F Y
Y J S O L E X I H B E Q P O C Y U
Q I N S T B O G F R E Z L J H C B
```

BELIEVER	HOPE	TEMPTATION
FORGIVENESS	HUMILITY	TESTIMONY
HEALING	PEACE	TRANSFORMATION

THE IMPACT OF PRAYER
WORDSEARCH--ANSWER

	1	2	3	4	5	6	7	8	9	10	11	12	13	14	15	16	17
1	H	U	M	I	L	I	T	Y	T	S	V	R	X	T	C	Q	U
2	D	I	T	M	B	P	E	E	D	R	E	F	P	Q	Y	X	C
3	R	I	X	S	P	I	P	S	C	P	P	A	H	N	D	K	E
4	R	O	X	I	S	X	W	Y	Y	A	W	J	O	P	S	T	U
5	R	O	A	H	S	A	H	H	V	Q	E	M	Y	H	R	X	N
6	R	B	F	E	E	Q	O	W	J	M	I	P	C	A	J	Q	U
7	N	I	U	A	N	C	A	Q	A	T	J	I	N	A	C	R	T
8	J	B	K	L	E	W	Q	R	S	P	X	S	C	N	N	F	A
9	G	L	L	I	V	C	V	E	O	A	F	E	O	W	L	J	L
10	X	W	G	N	I	I	T	J	W	O	F	I	N	P	L	Z	B
11	X	S	M	G	G	M	Z	E	R	W	T	B	O	C	R	E	M
12	C	N	X	D	R	T	M	M	P	A	H	O	P	E	L	M	U
13	U	V	E	Y	O	Z	A	J	T	G	V	H	F	I	A	E	J
14	T	F	U	V	F	T	Q	P	L	T	C	S	E	B	F	H	K
15	K	Y	Z	V	I	R	M	J	U	A	W	V	I	N	R	F	Y
16	Y	J	S	O	L	E	X	I	H	B	E	Q	P	O	C	Y	U
17	Q	I	N	S	T	B	O	G	F	R	E	Z	L	J	H	C	B

The words below are listed with their starting row and column

BELIEVER 10:17   HOPE 12:11   TEMPTATION 17:5

FORGIVENESS 14:5   HUMILITY 1:1   TESTIMONY 10:7

HEALING 5:4   PEACE 6:12   TRANSFORMATION 4:16

APPENDIX

GLOSSARY OF PRAYER TERMS

GLOSSARY

Adoration: A form of prayer that praises God for His greatness and acknowledges His majesty.

Amen: A word used at the end of a prayer meaning "so be it" or "truly."

Anointing: The act of applying oil in a religious ceremony, symbolizing consecration or divine blessing.

Apostle: One of the early followers of Jesus who was sent out to preach the gospel.

Assurance: Confidence in God's promises and faithfulness, often experienced through prayer.

Benediction: A short invocation for divine help, blessing, and guidance, usually at the end of a worship service.

Blessing: A prayer asking for God's favour and protection.

Calling: A strong inner impulse toward a particular course of action, especially when accompanied by conviction of divine influence.

Church: A community of believers who gather for worship, prayer, and fellowship.

Comfort: A sense of peace and reassurance provided by God through prayer

Communion: The sharing or exchanging of intimate thoughts and feelings with God, often involving the Eucharist.

Confession: Admitting sins to God in prayer and seeking His forgiveness.

Contemplation: A form of deep, reflective prayer focused on the presence of God.

Covenant: A solemn agreement between God and His people.

Cross: The symbol of Jesus' crucifixion and a central focus of Christian prayer and faith.

Devotion: Dedicated time spent in prayer and worship.

Discernment: The ability to understand or interpret God's will, often sought through prayer.

Disciple: A follower of Jesus, committed to learning from and living according to His teachings.

Encounter: A direct, personal experience of God during prayer.

Entreaty: An earnest or urgent request made in prayer.

Eternity: The timeless state of existence that believers look forward to with God.

Exalt: To praise and worship God with high regard.

Faith: Complete trust or confidence in God, often expressed through prayer.

Faithfulness: The quality of being loyal and steadfast, both as a characteristic of God and a desired trait in believers.

Fasting: Voluntarily abstaining from food, and sometimes other activities, to focus on prayer and spiritual growth.

Fellowship: The sharing of experiences and support among believers, often facilitated through communal prayer.

Forgiveness: The act of absolving someone of his/her sins, a key aspect of prayer.

Gospel: The teachings of Christ and the revelation of God's salvation through Him.

Grace: The free and unmerited favour of God, often sought and thanked for in prayer.

Gratitude: Thankfulness expressed to God in prayer.

Guidance: Seeking direction from God in prayer.

Healing: Physical, emotional, or spiritual recovery.

Holy: Sacred, set apart for God's purpose; a key focus in adoration and worship prayers.

Hope: Confident expectation of what God has promised, supported by faith and prayer.

Humility: The quality of being humble, recognizing one's need for God, often a posture in prayer.

Hymn: A song of praise to God, often used in prayer and worship.

Intercession: Praying on behalf of others.

Invocation: A prayer asking for God's presence and blessing.

Jesus: The central figure of Christianity, whose life and teachings are the foundation of Christian prayer. The acknowledged Son of God.

Joy: A feeling of great pleasure and happiness in God's presence, often experienced through prayer.

Kneel: A posture of humility and reverence in prayer.

Lament: A prayer expressing sorrow, mourning, or regret.

Listening: The practice of being silent and attentive to God's voice in prayer.

Lord's Prayer: The prayer Jesus taught His disciples, serving as a model for all Christian prayer.

Meditation: Focused reflection in prayer, often on scripture or a specific attribute of God.

Mercy: Compassion or forgiveness shown by God, often sought in prayer.

Miracles: Extraordinary events manifesting divine intervention, often a subject of prayer.

Obedience: Following God's commands, often strengthened through prayer.

Offering: A gift or sacrifice presented to God in prayer.

Peace: A state of tranquility and rest in God, often a result of prayer.

Petition: Asking God for specific needs or desires in prayer.

Praise: Expressing admiration and worship of God in prayer.

Presence: The sense of God's nearness during prayer.

Promise: God's assurances to His people, often a source of hope in prayer.

Protection: Asking God for safety and security in prayer.

Quiet: Silence or stillness in prayer, focusing on God's presence.

Reflection: Thoughtful consideration of one's life and relationship with God, often during prayer.

Repentance: Sincere regret or remorse for sin, coupled with a commitment to change, expressed in prayer.

Request: Asking God for specific blessings or help in prayer.

Reverence: Deep respect and awe for God, often expressed in prayer.

Sacred: Holy and set apart for God's purposes, often a focus in prayer.

Sacrifice: Offering something valuable to God in prayer.

Salvation: Deliverance from sin and its consequences, a central theme in Christian prayer.

Sanctification: The process of becoming more like Christ, often pursued through prayer.

Scripture: The holy writings of Christianity, often used in prayer.

Seek: To pursue God earnestly in prayer.

Serenity: A state of peace and calm in God's presence, often sought in prayer.

Silence: A period of quietness in prayer, focusing on listening to God.

Solitude: Being alone with God in prayer.

Song: A musical expression of prayer and worship.

Spirit: The Holy Spirit, who guides and empowers believers in prayer.

Strength: Spiritual fortitude gained through prayer.

Supplication: Earnestly and humbly asking for God's help in prayer.

Surrender: Yielding to God's will in prayer.

Thanksgiving: Expressing gratitude to God in prayer.

Tranquility: A state of peace and calm achieved through prayer.

Transformation: The process of spiritual change and growth through prayer.

Trust: Reliance on God's faithfulness, often reinforced through prayer.

Unity: Oneness among believers, often a focus in corporate prayer.

Vigil: A period of keeping awake for prayer, often during the night.

Voice: Speaking to God in prayer.

Vows: Promises made to God in prayer.

Waiting: Patiently seeking God's timing and direction in prayer.

War Room: A dedicated space for focused and strategic prayer.

Wholeness: Complete well-being, often sought through prayer.

Wisdom: Godly insight and understanding, often sought in prayer.

Worship: Adoring and revering God, often through prayer.

Yearning: Deep longing for God's presence, expressed in prayer.

Zeal: Passionate devotion to God, often reflected in prayer.

www.ingramcontent.com/pod-product-compliance
Lightning Source LLC
Chambersburg PA
CBHW051544010526
44118CB00022B/2577